I0827435

KEEPING THE PEACE WITHIN

FOLLOWING JESUS AS A FIRST RESPONDER

CLINT HATCH

Published by Innovo Publishing, LLC
www.innovopublishing.com
1-888-546-2111

Innovo Publishing LLC is a Christ-centered publisher located near Memphis, TN. Since 2008, Innovo has published quality books, eBooks, audiobooks, music, screenplays, and online and physical curricula that support the Great Commission, equip believers, and help create a positive Christian worldview. Innovo's capabilities and global reach provide Christian authors, artists, and ministries access to the world for Christ. To learn more about Innovo Publishing, visit our website at innovopublishing.com. To connect with other Christian creatives and to learn best practices for creating, publishing, marketing, and selling Christian titles, visit the Christian Publishing Portal at cpportal.com.

Keeping the Peace Within
Following Jesus as a First Responder

***This book contains descriptions of traumatic events and sensitive subject matter that may be disturbing to some readers. Reader discretion is advised.*

Library of Congress Control Number: 2026904028
ISBN: 979-8-88928-145-0

Cover Design & Interior Layout: Innovo Publishing, LLC

Printed in the United States of America
U.S. Printing History
First Edition: 2026

Dedicated to all my fellow first responders. I'm honored to be among your ranks. The journey to peace is worth it.

Don't give up!

CONTENTS

FOREWORD

May the words of my mouth and the meditation of my heart be pleasing to you, O LORD, my rock and my redeemer.

—PSALM 19:14

This book is a modest attempt to aid God's hungry children so to find Him. Nothing here is new except in the sense that it is a discovery which my own heart has made of spiritual realities most delightful and wonderful to me. Others before me have gone much farther into these holy mysteries than I have done, but if my fire is not large, it is yet real, and there may be those who can light their candle at its flame.

—A. W. Tozer, *The Pursuit of God*[1]

This quote from A. W. Tozer captures the heart of what I hope this book will be. I'm not the smartest, most experienced, or most impressive person—but I do love Jesus and long to follow Him more closely every day. Out of that faith, God has given me a deep desire to see my brothers and sisters in the first responder profession come to know Him. Having served in law enforcement for over twenty years, I've seen firsthand the weight we carry and the toll it takes. Because of those experiences, I feel compelled to share the truths God has shown me.

Faith in Jesus is foundational to the daily life of a first responder. It provides confidence and peace in the face of danger, strength to endure the hardest situations, and rest that allows us to be healthy, productive, and encouraging at

1. A. W. Tozer, *The Pursuit of God* (Harrisburg, PA: Christian Publications, 1948). Used with permission.

home and on the job. I cannot stress enough how vital faith is—it makes me want to grab every first responder and wake them up to the life-changing power of trusting in Jesus. I pray this book can be an alarm God uses to awaken people from their spiritual slumber!

Turning from sin, trusting that Jesus's work on the cross has cleansed you, believing that His resurrection gives you new life, and knowing that He sends His Holy Spirit to live inside you to help you follow Him—these are truths every person needs. But for first responders, who face evil and tragedy on a regular basis, I believe they are especially vital. Following Jesus isn't easy, but it is the only path to lasting meaning and true purpose in life.

> *Then Jesus said, "Come to me, all of you who are weary and carry heavy burdens, and I will give you rest. Take my yoke upon you. Let me teach you, because I am humble and gentle at heart, and you will find rest for your souls. For my yoke is easy to bear, and the burden I give you is light."*
>
> —Matthew 11:28-30

There was a time in my life when I lived my way, convinced I knew best—but really, I was just doing whatever I wanted. I grew up in church, yet I was far from God. Knowing about heaven didn't stop me from living like hell. But when everything came crashing down and all I had left was Jesus, it became a wake-up call that changed me in many ways.

My goal in this book is to speak directly and honestly to first responders. We're trained to handle other people's crises, yet we often neglect our own. Day after day, we face the evil, brokenness, and darkest parts of humanity, but we convince ourselves we won't be affected—that we're strong enough to carry it all. My prayer is that you'll see our true first response must always be to run to the Father, into His open and loving arms. From that relationship with God, and through the power of the Holy Spirit, we can confront the sin in our own lives and then serve others from a place of strength and health.

I want you to see the life-and-death struggle we face from a spiritual perspective. In the first responder community, conversations about mental health have thankfully become more open and honest. But if we don't view mental health through the lens of faith, we risk running in circles—talking about the problems without ever finding true hope or lasting solutions.

> *The soul is healed through union with Christ. In fact, to heal the soul without Jesus Christ is actually the process we ought to be calling into question. To help people to a better life without God is to help them away from God and into further independence from him.*
>
> *Jesus is available to every person, anywhere on the planet, any time. That is the Gospel and it is truly good news.*
>
> —John Eldredge, *Experience Jesus. Really.*[2]

I'm far from perfect—just ask my family, and they'll answer before you finish the question! I've struggled, but Jesus has changed me and continues to change me. I'm not who I used to be—and that's a good thing. Once you've experienced the new life the Spirit gives, you won't want to go back, no matter what challenges come your way.

2. Taken from *Experience Jesus. Really.* by John Eldredge Copyright © 2025 by John Eldredge. Used by permission of HarperCollins Christian Publishing. www.harpercollinschristian.com.

In these pages, I write primarily from a law enforcement perspective, but what I share will resonate with all first responders. Our roles may differ, yet we face many of the same challenges. My goal is to show what it looks like to practically follow Jesus in this line of work. Even if you're not a first responder, I believe you'll find truths to apply—and perhaps gain insight into the world your spouse, family member, or friend lives in every day. You'll read life stories and work experiences that are sometimes raw, though I've left out the more graphic details. As first responders, we have a front-row seat to the worst of humanity, and we all carry the weight of difficult calls and cases. My desire is to give you a glimpse into this life while pointing to the foundation we need most: following Jesus in our careers and in every part of our lives.

I'll be drawing on a lot of Scripture to show how God's Word speaks directly to our daily lives in practical ways.

> *For the word of God is alive and powerful. It is sharper than the sharpest two-edged sword, cutting between soul and spirit, between joint and marrow. It exposes our innermost thoughts and desires.*
>
> —Hebrews 4:12

I've included reflection questions and a personal prayer at the end of each chapter to help you pause, process, and deepen your relationship with the Lord. My hope is that we'll be freed from the weight of sin, moved by the needs of others, and fueled by a desire to serve and protect our communities—living healthy, whole lives that flow from knowing we are loved and accepted by God.

To my fellow first responders: until the cornerstone of Jesus is set firmly under your feet, you're building on sand. Don't just take my word for it—trust, but verify. Investigate for yourself. I'll lay out my case, and then you can decide what you'll do with Jesus. Join me on this journey, and let's fight to keep the peace within.

> *"Peace I leave you, My peace I give you; not as the world gives, do I give to you. Do not let your hearts be troubled, nor fearful."*
> —Jesus in John 14:27

PRAYER

Father, I pray for the person reading this book. That You would open their eyes to see You, open their ears to hear You, and soften their hearts to feel You. Grant them an understanding of the truth that only comes from You, and help them to know You deeply and personally by drinking from the well of life so they may thirst no more. May they experience true peace that only You can give. In Jesus's name and by the power of the Holy Spirit, Amen.

Chapter 1
IDENTITY

Therefore, if anyone is in Christ, he is a new creation. The old has passed away; behold, the new has come.

—2 Corinthians 5:17 ESV

No matter the damage, no matter the story, the soul is healed through union with Christ.

—John Eldredge, *Experience Jesus. Really.*[3]

It was late one night on shift when we got the call from the renter of an apartment. They couldn't open the door because it was barricaded from the inside. They had no idea who could be in there. A few other officers and I responded and banged on the door, announcing ourselves before we forced the front door open. We probably didn't use the most

3. Taken from *Experience Jesus. Really.* by John Eldredge Copyright © 2025 by John Eldredge. Used by permission of HarperCollins Christian Publishing. www.harpercollinschristian.com.

tactically sound methods, but we were pumped up and ready to go.

The couch, among other things, had been put up against the door to block it. We were able to push the door open enough for me to get my weapon inside to clear the area so we didn't get shot through the door. Once we forced the door open enough to get inside, we started to work on clearing the apartment and locating the person or people inside. *Clearing* a residential area like that requires communication and teamwork so that you cover your partner while they are checking another section of the apartment. We didn't hear anything inside, so we methodically worked our way through the apartment until we came to the back bedroom with a closed door. We checked the door and discovered it was unlocked, so we opened it and saw a person lying in bed with the covers pulled up so that just his head was showing. Crazily enough he seemed to be asleep, and there was a pistol on the nightstand right next to the guy.

We had been making a lot of noise announcing that we were police officers, so my first thought was that he was faking being asleep, and he was going to do something soon. I spoke loud enough to wake him up, and he slowly opened his eyes. He looked at me with wide eyes, and I immediately told him to slowly take his hands out from underneath the covers. I let him know we were aware of the gun beside him, and if he moved toward it, he was going to get shot. Thankfully, he did as he was told, and we were able to place him under arrest. Later we discovered, upon closer inspection, the gun was just a pellet gun. Even after identifying the guy, the renter of the apartment still had no clue who he was. Looking back, I believe he was having a mental health crisis, but he was charged with breaking and entering. This was back before mental health was as understood as it is today. I hope he was able to get the help he needed.

This is one story of many in my career where I had to work together with others on my shift, in a high-stress environment, to accomplish a shared goal. These kinds of events can really solidify identity and purpose in the first responder profession. Just in this story alone, there were many things that could've gone wrong. There could've been more than one person in the apartment, the gun could've been real and we could've been shot at through the door, we could have been injured or had to injure the guy there in order to get the situation under control. Facing the inherent dangers together and coming out the other side can really bring you together. That sense of family is strong within the first responder world.

THE POWER OF BELONGING

Life and work within this profession has shaped the person I've become—for better or worse. First responder work has definitely changed how I view the general public. Growing up, I had a basic trust for people and an idea that bad things happen, but being a police officer has opened my eyes to the depravity of humanity. Since most people can't relate to what we see and do as first responders, we tend to identify and relate easily with those in our own profession. I don't think that's unusual with any job, but, in my experience, it's especially true with law enforcement and other first responders. Graduating from the Police Academy and becoming a certified law enforcement officer is a rite of passage into a tight-knit group of like-minded people.

My first day at the Police Academy is one I'll never forget. I had heard stories about how it would be, but experiencing it was another thing entirely. We had just finished the preliminary physicals and, although I didn't know it, were about to be welcomed to the Mississippi Law Enforcement Training Academy (MLEOTA) in Pearl, MS.

Suddenly, the people in charge were yelling at us, calling us knuckleheads, and making us do push-ups, jumping jacks, and mountain climbers for no reason. I distinctly remember my primary instructor reminding us that we were just knucklehead recruits who had better not make eye contact with him and were not allowed to talk to him directly. If we wanted to speak to him, we had to voice our concerns to his hand first. The instructions for that lovely process were as follows:

> Knucklehead recruit: SIR, PERMISSION TO SPEAK TO THE HAND, SIR!
>
> Instructor throwing his open hand up inches in front of your face: BAM!

We'd have to try and get our thoughts together while "fearing for our life" and make our request fully known to his hand.

Oh, sure . . . it's funny now. Back then we were just trying not to die from physical exercises or, as we called it, trying not to *get smoked.* I call it physical exercises, but it was really just whatever the instructors wanted us to do that would make life miserable.

The first night I laid down on that hard, short mattress with my head on that flat pillow, I distinctly remember looking up at the ceiling and thinking to myself, *What in the world have I gotten myself into?* I didn't sleep well, and I was worried whether I was even going to make the cut. After that night, however, I made up my mind I was going to get through this. I really didn't have an option, though, after having just gotten married a couple of months earlier, and this being the only job opportunity on the table. If I didn't make it, I would be newly married and out of work. Talk about motivation!

Another memory I have of the Police Academy is a six-mile formation run around one of our state's correctional facilities. We ran early in the morning, before sunrise, and everyone participated in various cadences—loudly. I'm sure the correction officers hated us because it would rile the inmates up. We could hear them yelling from inside the prison walls. The one cadence from that time that always stuck with me was, "Freedom! Get some!" I wonder why the inmates didn't like that one?

I can vividly remember keeping in step with my platoon, panting but hyped up, and screaming that at the top of my lungs, thinking, *I'm on the right side of the law, and they're on the wrong side. I'm one of the good guys, and they're the bad guys.* It felt so cut and dry in the moment. It wasn't until I started following Jesus when I realized my soul had been imprisoned for years. Jesus had been offering His "Freedom!" and urging me to "Get some!"—but I had been yelling at Him with my life to shut up and go away. And yet His "goodness and unfailing love will pursue me all the days of my life" (Psalm 23:6).

As I look back, I realize that's where my identity really started to become ingrained in me as a law enforcement officer. I was a police officer, and this is the group I belong to. This is who I am. Have you felt that way? Everyone finds their identity in something, and the first responder profession is such an easy transition because you are actually doing something with like-minded people that matters and helps the community.

After completing the academy, reality hit, and I was thrown into the muck and mire of humanity where, suddenly, things that seemed black and white shift to gray, and I was left wondering how to deal with them. I had a college degree and had just graduated from the Police Academy, but when I put that uniform on and started my first night on patrol, I felt like a fish out of water. All my education and training were being practically put to the test. I am a firm believer in on-the-job training. That's where you truly learn and can actually put into practice any knowledge you have.

My first night on patrol was definitely eye-opening. I was the new guy and had to learn the paperwork process, the computer systems, the way to put what I learned into action, etc. "Like drinking from a fire hose," they would say.

It was a lot.

My field training officer (FTO) put me in the passenger seat and wouldn't even let me drive. The call I remember from my first night was someone stealing gas from one of the convenience stores. He filled up his vehicle and left without paying. The call came out with a vehicle description, and we were close by. We got to the area as quickly as we could and spotted the vehicle passing us, going the other way, trying to get out of our jurisdiction and into the large city that bordered us. We made a quick U-turn and got behind the vehicle. My FTO checked the tag as we were about to pull the vehicle over, and our dispatcher let us know the vehicle was stolen. He hit the lights and sirens after backup fell in behind us, and the vehicle pulled over into a large parking lot. We swooped in front of the vehicle with my side, the passenger side, facing the front of the vehicle. I sarcastically thanked my FTO later for putting me on that side. I guess he was just using me as a human shield. I remember seeing the guy's scared face as we all jumped out and held him at gunpoint until someone could get him handcuffed. As all first responders know, the fun didn't last long before we got swamped with paperwork, but it was a memorable first night shift.

All jokes aside, I am truly grateful for my FTO. I was as green as could be when I first started, and he was a no-nonsense kind of guy. After I had been on the FTO program for a little while and had begun to kind of stall out, he said, "If you don't take some initiative and get things done, you're not going to make it." He gave me the much-needed kick in the butt that set me onto a great career path. I am indebted to his desire to train me and get my feet firmly set before releasing me into the wild.

Once you get a few on-the-job stories like that under your belt, you feel accepted and needed within a community of people striving toward the same mission. I felt this strongly, and since I wanted to please everyone during that time of my life, I fell into the good and bad that comes with law enforcement. I found my identity as a first responder.

Here are some of the thoughts I've had over the years:

- *I'm a first responder, and no one really understands me except others in my profession.*
- *I'm part of this larger group of people, and we're in this together.*
- *I can't trust anyone except other first responders.*
- *Being a first responder is who I am and what defines me.*
- *I can't talk to anyone about what I've seen and had to do.*
- *I have to keep all these things I've experienced inside and deal with them myself.*

These kinds of thoughts really affected my life in ways I didn't understand until later. They changed me, affecting my marriage and social life. No one really understands what it's like to be anybody else, but we can still be there for each other, support each other, and find a better way to deal with these issues than what we've been doing in the past. The Bible puts it this way:

> *Share each other's burdens, and in this way obey the law of Christ.*
>
> –Galatians 6:2

Your identity is not in your job, title, position, experiences, or anything else. All of those things will pass away eventually. What are you going to do then? When you no longer work as a dispatcher, firefighter, paramedic, police officer, etc.?

We must find our identity in something that will never pass away. Something eternal.

We must find our identity in Jesus.

Once we have Him as our foundation, we can build a life that will not be shaken.

THE REALITY OF THE PROFESSION

I think we, as first responders, are finally beginning to realize how we need to take better care of ourselves for the sake of the people we serve and our friends and families, but we still have some work to do.

A quick internet search on traumatic events among first responders reveals a great deal. Research consistently shows that the traumatic situations they encounter on a regular basis can have significant negative effects on their lives. We constantly respond to emergencies, not realizing that the job is creating an emergency in our own lives. It leaves us exposed to many issues we don't like to talk about (PTSD, suicide, divorce, addiction, etc.) but are very prominent in the first responder profession. Many first responders want to feel normal but end up feeling isolated, thinking they're the only ones dealing with these problems. We can end up suffering in silence for too long. Statistics show first responders experience over 200 percent more traumatic experiences than the average person in a thirty-year career and are at a higher risk of developing various mental health conditions. However, the actual number of first responders suffering from these conditions may be undercounted because they tend to avoid conversations about their experiences. There can unfortunately be a stigma associated with these issues and conversations, so we tend to just ignore it and try to deal with it ourselves.[4,5,6]

If we are to healthily navigate this treacherous but fulfilling profession of service to our community, we must have a firm grasp of our faith and identity in Christ and the power of the Holy Spirit in our lives. We are going to delve more into the relationship we can have with Jesus through faith, but there are a few questions I'd like you to ask yourself before moving on. Take your time, and answer honestly.

QUESTIONS

- What do I actually place my faith in? (Is it money, status, a relationship, myself, etc.?)

- Am I healthy? (mentally, physically, spiritually, emotionally?)

4. M. G. Quirke, "Key Statistics About PTSD in First Responders," *michaelgquirke.com*, accessed 2005, https://michaelgquirke.com/key-statistics-about-ptsd-in-first-responders/

5. R. Zemlok, "How Ongoing Traumatic Exposures Impact First Responders," *Police1.com*, January 12, 2023, accessed [insert access date], https://www.police1.com/health-wellness/articles/how-ongoing-traumatic-exposures-impact-first-responders-IKu7UkIsm2SqWtXB/

6. C. H. Cannady, "Suicidology Among First Responders: A Literature Review of Causal and Protective Factors," *Cummings Graduate Institute for Behavioral Health Studies*, March 5, 2024, accessed [insert access date], https://cgi.edu/news/suicidology-among-first-responders-a-literature-review-of-causal-and-protective-factors/

- How are my relationships? (family, friends, coworkers?)

- Where do I find my identity? (job, what kind of person I am, what I can do, who I know?)

PRAYER

Jesus, help me to find my identity in You alone and not in anything or anyone else, including myself. Continue to soften my heart and help me realize I need You more than I need the breath in my lungs. Prepare my heart, and give me an open mind to receive Your truths as I walk through the rest of this book. I want to seek You, and I desire to know You in a deeper way. It's in Your name I pray, Amen.

Chapter 2

THE SICKNESS AND THE ENEMY

Oh, what a miserable person I am! Who will free me from this life that is dominated by sin and death?

—Romans 7:24

Neither the writer nor the reader of these words is qualified to appreciate the holiness of God. Quite literally a new channel must be cut through the desert of our minds to allow the sweet waters of truth that will heal our great sickness to flow in.

—A. W. Tozer, *The Knowledge of the Holy*[7]

This chapter could be difficult for you, depending on where you are spiritually. However, I think we would all agree that in order for us to find the right solution, we need

7. A. W. Tozer, *The Knowledge of the Holy* (New York: HarperCollins, 1961).

to know what the problem is. You wouldn't want your doctor just giving you random medication until he finds out what works. You want him to know the issue first so he can have a proper diagnosis to be able to find the right medication for you.

That's kind of like what I want to try to do with this chapter—to show the sickness we all share and reveal the enemy of our souls so we can clearly see the cure and victory offered to all of us.

As a first responder, I felt like I had a pretty good grasp of good and evil and considered myself on the right side of the battle. We do see evil more than most people. From the time the call comes in to dispatch, to the response in the field, to reliving it while filing the report, to finalizing cases and taking it to court, we are inundated with the evil, depravity, and sickness of humanity, and we just assume we're able to deal with all that we have to see and do—like our profession is just a regular job. We just went over the stats showing how an average person will experience a few traumatic events in their lifetime, but first responders experience traumatic events regularly due to the job we have to do.

The first dead body I saw was an infant who died in the night from sudden infant death syndrome (SIDS). Trying to process that and also help the shocked and grieving couple was difficult. The first suicide I saw was the result of a call from a concerned family member who just wanted us to go check on their loved one. As we checked through the young lady's house to see if she was there, I opened her closet door, turned on the light, and she was hanging there right in front of me. The first death notification I did was to let a mother know her teenage son, who was high on marijuana and other substances, had been crushed by his vehicle after it veered off the road and flipped over in a ditch. I stumbled through the words as I delivered the heartbreaking news to his mother.

These are just a few of the calls I've dealt with, and I know I haven't experienced half of what other first responders have. This isn't to gain sympathy but to take an honest look at the reality of the profession and what we're dealing with on a daily basis.

Because of all the stress that comes with the job, we tend to find illegitimate ways to alleviate that stress—be it alcohol, sex, drugs (legal and illegal), anger, relationships, etc. Pick your poison. Whatever helps you deal with . . .

- the memory of the bloated dead body that was stuck to the carpet.
- the burned corpse that you stumbled upon while putting out a fire.
- the person who died on the stretcher even after all you tried to do.
- the person who took their own life even after you tried to talk them down.
- someone's life you had to end in order to save your life or the life of someone else.

Being in public service is being right in the middle of the worst of humanity. Because of all we have to deal with and because it's a worthy cause, it can make us think we're getting extra credit with the "Man upstairs." We're "serving and protecting," and that has to count for something, right? We think we need or deserve a break from all the carnage and chaos, so we gravitate toward all these things that numb the pain, things that give us temporary relief but end up making things worse in the long run.

Everyone has a past and personal struggles as well, so if you add that in with the unique stress from being a first responder, you get a dangerous cocktail of emotions. If left to our own devices, we're headed down a wide road of destruction.

> *"You can enter God's Kingdom only through the narrow gate. The highway to hell is broad, and its gate is wide for the many who choose that way. But the gateway to life is very narrow and the road is difficult, and only a few ever find it."*
> —MATTHEW 7:13-14

Regarding illegitimate ways of coping with life or stress, C. S. Lewis had some interesting takes in his books *The Weight of Glory* and *Mere Christianity*.[8,9] He brings out the point that our desires are basically being focused in the wrong direction—toward alcohol, sex, ambition, etc. He compares it to a child wanting to keep making mud pies in a state of poverty because they can't imagine what a vacation at the beach would be like. We settle for so much less in our lives. Lewis goes on to make the point that if we feel like there is something missing in our lives this natural world can't fulfill, then maybe there's a supernatural explanation. Maybe we're looking for created things to fill the void inside our souls when we should be looking to the Creator of all things to make us whole.

THE COMMON STRUGGLE

I definitely struggled with this early on in my career—trying to find my identity in my profession, trying to please everyone, trying to be perfect, and trying to deal with the stress and trauma in illegitimate ways (while trying to hide the fact that I'm dealing with the stress and trauma in illegitimate ways). I filled my life with all the things this world offered to try to find purpose and joy. I was also carrying around some trauma from earlier childhood experiences that I didn't realize affected me as much as it did. It all led me down a dark road

8. C. S. Lewis, *The Weight of Glory*, rev. ed. (New York: Macmillan, 1980).
9. C. S. Lewis, *Mere Christianity*, rev. ed. (New York: Macmillan, 1952).

I almost didn't come back from. These are not excuses but confessions to try and understand the root of the problem.

Throughout my life and early into my law enforcement career, I would've told you I was a Christian, but if you really knew how I lived, you wouldn't have been able to believe it. One look at the fruit of my life and you would have known I was dead in my sin and in need of a Savior. A hypocrite of the highest order! I began struggling with keeping my *good* mask on and maintaining the facade of being a *really good Christian.* What people thought of me (pleasing people), the fear of man, anger, and the lusts of the flesh (pornography) were very real struggles for me. The vice grip of sin and evil had been choking me for a long time, and I never truly realized it.

I didn't understand how deeply the sin, childhood trauma, and work-related trauma affected me until I hit rock bottom. I eventually landed in a dark place where I felt like the only answer was to end it all. I had my duty pistol in my mouth, finger on the trigger, and tears streaming down my face, trying to work up enough courage to stop the madness and chaos inside of me. I was only twenty-four years old at the time, two years into marriage and a career, ready and willing to cut my life short. I didn't see any other way out and felt completely hopeless.

Looking back at that moment really brings the truth out of the following verses:

> *Stay alert! Watch out for your great enemy, the devil. He prowls around like a roaring lion, looking for someone to devour.*
>
> —1 Peter 5:8

> *"The thief comes only to steal and kill and destroy. I came that they may have life and have it abundantly."*
>
> —John 10:10 ESV

I feel like I do need to clarify that the childhood trauma mentioned above was not from my family—thankfully. I know so many people deal with that, but I don't want to misrepresent what happened. My parents were amazing. Not perfect, but I knew I was loved and provided for. Something a lot of people don't have. They kept us in church where we heard the truth, and I know they prayed for my brother and me all the time. God used the spiritual foundation they laid and my parents' prayers to establish my faith in Jesus, in spite of everything the world and Satan tried to throw at me. The truth of the following verse is evident in my life:

> *Direct your children onto the right path, and when they are older, they will not leave it.*
>
> —Proverbs 22:6

Another truth I've realized over the course of my life is that no matter how good of an upbringing you had, you're still dead in sin and in need of a Savior. Besides the sin in our lives, which we will talk about next, we have a very real enemy in Satan. Like the verses quoted previously, he is unseen but a very real power in this world, and he hates your guts. So many times we get angry or frustrated at people and events in our lives and don't realize it could be a spiritual attack from the devil and his demons.

> *We are not fighting against flesh-and-blood enemies, but against evil rulers and authorities of the unseen world, against mighty powers in this dark world, and against evil spirits in the heavenly places.*
>
> —Ephesians 6:12

This is why it's so important to look under the surface of things and get to the root of the issue. First responders know this all too well. We see people at their worst, and I truly believe there have been many times where I have dealt with demonic forces, and God helped me through it. Whatever you struggle with, look deeper to see what the true cause of it could be. It could be an unseen power or spirit coming against you. These attacks are so easily overlooked because they're not part of our perceived reality, and that's what makes it so dangerous. Get help from a trusted Christian counselor, or open up to a trusted friend who you know loves and follows Jesus. As we'll see in the next chapter, once you turn and follow Jesus, He gives you power over these forces, but until then, you're incredibly vulnerable. Thankfully, my loving Heavenly Father interceded and saved my life. I am so grateful God had other plans! But for God, I shudder to think of what would have been.

After realizing how bad things had gotten with me, I initially tried to do better, to change and make things right myself, but that never truly works in the long run. I finally came to the end of myself one night while working the night shift. I believe it was the Holy Spirit urging me to have honest conversations and genuine confessions with my wife and other trusted people in my life.

> *Confess your sins to each other and pray for each other so that you may be healed.*
>
> —James 5:16a

Along with the Spirit's urging came a heavy realization of the depths of my sin and the condition my soul was in. I knew I was dead in my sins and separated from my loving Heavenly Father. The truths I had been taught throughout my life suddenly became a reality to me, and I knew that without God's help, I would have no hope of survival. I felt this in a deeply personal way. I vividly remember working an overtime security detail one night, right after God convicted me to turn from my sins and trust in Jesus. I felt the impact my sins had on my life and my loved ones' lives. It shook me and made me very emotional to be fully aware of my sin while also experiencing the reality of God's grace and mercy in Jesus. It made me get out of my car, hit my knees, and look up at the sky. It was a clear night, and the stars were bright. I was struck with the greatness of God and how unworthy I was to receive His love. But He lavishes it on me nonetheless, solely because I trusted Jesus. Faith unleashed the fountain of God's love to wash over me.

> *Jesus paid it all,*
> *All to Him I owe;*
> *Sin had left a crimson stain,*
> *He washed it white as snow.*
> —Elvina M. Hall, "Jesus Paid It All"[10]

Now, some of you may be thinking to yourselves, *Wow! He's really messed up!* And, it's true, I was messed up in a lot of ways. Like Paul, I felt as if I was the worst—or "chief"—of sinners (1 Timothy 1:15), and I related to the man Jesus talked about who "dared not even lift his eyes to heaven as he prayed. Instead, he beat his chest in sorrow, saying, 'O God, be merciful to me, for I am a sinner'" (Luke 18:13). The truth is, we're all messed up. Our spirits are dead because of sin.

> *If we claim we have no sin, we are only fooling ourselves and not living in the truth. But if we confess our sins to him, he is faithful and just to forgive us our sins and to cleanse us from all wickedness.*
> —1 John 1:8-9

10. E. M. Hall, "Jesus Paid It All," in *Sabbath Carols Hymnal* (1865). Used with permission.

THE TRUTH ABOUT SIN

This issue of sin is something I really want to drill down on. It's a taboo topic in the world and not totally understood. The use of the word *sin* in the Bible has been translated in different ways but essentially boils down to an overall theme. According to an *Evidence for Christianity* post by Dr. John Oaks, the Bible conveys that God wants to confront not only our rebellious or purposeful sins but also the sins we do unintentionally. The way we can know what's right but willfully choose to do wrong or how we can just naturally miss the mark for what God desires for us.[11]

The word *sin* is also used in archery. When you miss the bullseye, or *miss the mark,* it's called a sin. The problem with us all is sin; however, when we think of sin, it's usually in the context of doing something bad or evil. It certainly is that, but it can also be good things we know we should do but don't, and good things we do for the wrong reasons.

> *For everyone has sinned; we all fall short of God's glorious standard.*
> —Romans 3:23

And because we have all rebelled against the Holy God and selfishly done our own thing, essentially making ourselves a god in our own eyes, we deserve death and eternal separation from God. With our lives we have told God, "I don't want You, and I don't need You. I want to be in charge."

> *For the wages of sin is death.*
> —Romans 6:23a

The word *wages* refers to payment for work—like we've done a great job of sinning against God, and the payment

11. J. Oaks, "What Are the Origins of the Word 'Sin'?" *Evidence for Christianity*, May 8, 2005, accessed 2005, https://evidenceforchristianity.org/what-are-the-origins-of-the-word-sinr/

for that is death. The pay we have rightfully earned from our work as people who do wrong and evil against our loving Heavenly Father is death. That is what we deserve—what we have earned.

A. W. Tozer puts it this way:

> *God's justice stands forever against the sinner in utter severity. The vague and tenuous hope that God is too kind to punish the ungodly has become a deadly opiate for the consciences of millions. It hushes their fears and allows them to practice all pleasant forms of iniquity while death draws every day nearer and the command to repent goes unregarded.*
>
> —A. W. Tozer, *The Knowledge of the Holy* [12]

I know this isn't fun to talk about sin and death, but you have to know the truth from God's Word. He wants to open your eyes to the hopeless situation your sin has you in so you'll realize your desperate need for a Savior.

I'm also trying to wake you up to the reality of what's happening around you. We're in a dire situation, and we need a truth alarm to wake us out of our distracted stupor. It would be wrong for me to withhold this truth. We're all in this together, and I am no different than you in that regard. If we are to truly grasp, appreciate, and begin to understand the Good News of Jesus, we have to be able to look truthfully inside ourselves and realize the depths of our depravity and how lost and dead we really are.

If you still think you're a pretty good person, go check out the Ten Commandments (found in Exodus 20 and Deuteronomy 5), and see how good you really are. The commandments are something we have all probably heard of or are at least somewhat familiar with. Be honest with yourself

12. A. W. Tozer, *The Knowledge of the Holy* (New York: HarperCollins, 1961).

and go through them to see how many you've kept and not broken at all. Not even once. The number of commandments you have kept will be easier to calculate because it won't be many—if any.

> *Yes indeed, it is good when you obey the royal law as found in the Scriptures: "Love your neighbor as yourself." But if you favor some people over others, you are committing a sin. You are guilty of breaking the law.* For the person who keeps all of the laws except one is as guilty as a person who has broken all of God's laws.
>
> —James 2:8-10, emphasis added

If we compare ourselves to other people, we will always find someone we feel is worse than we are. We can think, *Yeah, I'm not perfect, but I'm not as bad as that person over there, so I must be doing OK*—tending to see the sin in the streets but remaining blind to the sin inside of us. We need to start looking up and comparing ourselves to God, a holy and perfect God that even the angels hide their faces from (Isaiah 6:2). If we compare ourselves to God, then the truth of our sins can set in, and we can realize just how evil we are. It's similar to how white a sheep can look when it's grazing in the green grass, but put that same sheep in pure white snow and you'll see it's not as clean as you thought. If we compare ourselves to a holy God, we'll quickly see how sinful we are.

I've always thought of the Ten Commandments as laws I have to keep so that God will be happy with me. If I break them, God gets upset with me. I then have to ask God to forgive me and then try my best to keep the laws so I can go to heaven. This mindset is common, but it's just not true. The law is actually kind of like a mirror to show us how dirty we are. This is a way we can compare ourselves with God.

> *Why, then, was the law given? It was given alongside the promise to show people their sins.*
> —Galatians 3:19a

My wife and I have a good friend who has been a missionary in Papua New Guinea for several years. When teaching in villages, they often use this analogy of comparing God's law to a mirror. If we have dirt on our face, we can't see it, and even if others tell us we're dirty, we may not believe them. But if we hold God's laws up to our lives, we can see how dirty we are. Then, we might try to clean ourselves only to discover we can't do it. If we can understand that, it will push us to seek help. The temptation here, however, is to say something like, "Yeah, I know I've done some bad things, but God will forgive me, right?" Yes, there is a way to be forgiven, but we have to understand how that happens. Our Heavenly Father has said, "The Lord is slow to anger and filled with unfailing love, forgiving every kind of sin and rebellion. But he does not excuse the guilty" (Numbers 14:18a).

Because of where I grew up and my experiences, I try to cut through the American Bible Belt mentality of, "I believe in Jesus, and He will forgive me no matter what I do." Or, "I believe in Jesus and will do the best I can to stay in His good graces." These mindsets subtly place emphasis on either excusing the sinfulness in our lives or the good things we can do to please God and save ourselves.

Allow me a court analogy, if you will, since I'm in law enforcement. Let's say you did something bad, and you're in court before the judge. He declares you guilty, and you start asking for forgiveness—telling him you're sorry, that you'll never do it again, and you'll start doing better. The judge says, "Well, I'm glad you're sorry and wanting to do better, but you're still guilty, and justice must be served. I can't just forgive you and let you go. That wouldn't be legal or just." Nothing changes the fact that we have sinned against God. We have completely disrespected His authority and disregarded His honor. We stand before Him guilty as charged and deserving of our death sentence. That's how serious sin is to God. Someone must pay the penalty or it isn't legal or just.

This revelation should help us understand that we cannot fix or save ourselves. We have a mortal illness, and we need the cure. Once we truly realize this, we wonder if there's any hope. Thank the good Lord there is Good News!

Now that we've turned and faced the truth of our dire situation before God, we can truly appreciate the cure our Father offers to us. Let's dive headfirst into the amazing grace and new life Jesus offers for those who would believe.

QUESTIONS

- Do I know how sinful I am and in need of saving, or is there some hesitation?

- If there is some hesitation, what could be keeping me from seeing the truth?

PRAYER

Heavenly Father, help me to see my sin for what it truly is—death and destruction to me, and something You will not be in the presence of because of Your holiness. Give me a broken and tender heart over the ways I have rebelled and sinned against You alone, Lord. May my brokenness lead me to trust in You, Jesus. Amen.

Chapter 3

THE CURE

Oh, what a miserable person I am! Who will free me from this life that is dominated by sin and death? Thank God! The answer is in Jesus Christ our Lord.

—Romans 7:24-25a, emphasis added

One of my favorite "Bible" words is *propitiation,* which essentially means to appease God's wrath and turn it to favor. Let's look at the rest of the two verses mentioned in the previous chapter in that context.

> *For everyone has sinned; we all fall short of God's glorious standard. Yet God, in his grace, freely makes us right in his sight. He did this through Christ Jesus when he freed us from the penalty for our sins. For God presented Jesus as the sacrifice for sin. People are made right with God when they believe that Jesus sacrificed his life, shedding his blood.*
>
> —Romans 3:23-25a

For the wages of sin is death, but the free gift of God is eternal life through Christ Jesus our Lord.

—Romans 6:23

In Ephesians, Paul sums it up so well:

Once you were dead because of your disobedience and your many sins. You used to live in sin, just like the rest of the world, obeying the devil—the commander of the powers in the unseen world. He is the spirit at work in the hearts of those who refuse to obey God. All of us used to live that way, following the passionate desires and inclinations of our sinful nature. By our very nature we were subject to God's anger, just like everyone else.

But God is so rich in mercy, and he loved us so much, that even though we were dead because of our sins, he gave us life when he raised Christ from the dead. (It is only by God's grace that you have been saved!)

God saved you by his grace when you believed. And you can't take credit for this; it is a gift from God. Salvation is not a reward for the good things we have done, so none of us can boast about it. *For we are God's masterpiece. He has created us anew in Christ Jesus, so we can do the good things he planned for us long ago.*

—Ephesians 2:1-5, 8-10, emphasis added

God's wrath and justice against sin met with His love, grace, and mercy at the cross.

> *For God made Christ, who never sinned, to be the offering for our sin, so that we could be made right with God through Christ.*
> —2 Corinthians 5:21

Let's go back to the court example I posed in the previous chapter. You're guilty before the judge, and, just before he sentences you, Jesus steps in and says, "I'm taking his place. He gets my freedom, and I get his sentence." If you place your trust in Jesus to save you, then the gavel of God's wrath slams down on Jesus instead of you.

> *So now there is no condemnation for those who belong to Christ Jesus.*
> —Romans 8:1

This is an incredible exchange. Jesus, as God in human form, died our death so we can live His life! It is such an amazing, life-altering revelation. There was no way we could save ourselves, so God did it for us. All that is required of us is to accept the free gift God has offered us.

We spent the whole last chapter wading through the consequences of sin and death. May we say "no!" to sin and "yes!" to Jesus. The hell that has been waiting for us has been conquered in the name of Jesus!

The truths about sin and Jesus are foundational to faith in Jesus. I struggled with it myself. I had been taught the truths of Christianity my whole life but never really stopped to consider what that meant. Faith was a part of my family but not a part of me. It was only when I hit rock bottom with the collision of life and faith that I took a hard look at my own beliefs. When you're put between a rock and a hard place, the truth of what you believe comes bleeding through. I looked at Creation and my consciousness and knew there had to be a God. All the other religions talk about the good things you can do to try and earn God's favor, but God showed me even my "righteous deeds are nothing but filthy rags" (Isaiah 64:6). Even the good things we do are tainted with wrong motives and selfish reasons.

With the depth of my sin on full display and knowing I could never tip the scales in my favor before a holy God, I fell on His grace and mercy in Jesus. Once we turn from our sins and begin following Jesus, He sends the Holy Spirit into our lives to help us, just like He promised. We'll talk more about that, but Jesus knows how tough life can be. That's why He sent the Spirit as a helper and guide for us.

Hopefully you can see that turning from sin to faith and identity in Jesus are the most important parts of life here and in eternity—that it is only through faith we can please God, have purpose in this life, and be effective at our calling. It's crucial for our life, family, and career as a first responder.

Some other questions to consider are,

1. Where do we start?
2. Who exactly is Jesus?
3. What does it mean to place my faith and trust in Him?

WHERE DO WE START?

There are many, way more educated people out there who can better explain and advocate on the logic and evidence behind the Christian faith. I am a simple kind of man. The kind Lynyrd Skynyrd sang about. I like how Jesus explained it:

> *About that time the disciples came to Jesus and asked, "Who is greatest in the Kingdom of Heaven?" Jesus called a little child to him and put the child among them. Then he said, "I tell you the truth, unless you turn from your sins*

> *and become like little children, you will never get into the Kingdom of Heaven. So anyone who becomes as humble as this little child is the greatest in the Kingdom of Heaven."*
> —Matthew 18:1-4

Just look at the world around us—from the grandeur of space to the microscopic tapestry that holds it all together. We inherently know there is a Creator behind all of this.

> *They know the truth about God because he has made it obvious to them. For ever since the world was created, people have seen the earth and sky. Through everything God made, they can clearly see his invisible qualities—his eternal power and divine nature. So they have no excuse for not knowing God.*
> —Romans 1:19-20

We need to develop awe and wonder like a child discovering something for the first time. They can't contain their excitement! A building points to an architect, a painting points to an artist, a book points to an author, and creation points us to the Creator. A Creator who loves us and wants us to be with Him forever. If that's true, then how do we know God? Out of all the world religions, there is only one that claims God came to save us because we couldn't save ourselves. Every other religion, even atheism, places the responsibility of salvation squarely on our shoulders. However, if you have been running on the hamster wheel of good works, you know you're fighting a losing battle. This is the simple but vital difference between Christianity and all other world religions.

The truth is this:

> *Jesus told him, "I am the way, the truth, and the life. No one can come to the Father except through me."*
> —John 14:6

And Peter declared, by the power of the Holy Spirit,

> *"For Jesus is the one referred to in the Scriptures, where it says, 'The stone that you builders rejected has now become the cornerstone.' There is salvation in no one else! God has given no other name under heaven by which we must be saved."*
> —Acts 4:11-12

WHO IS JESUS?

So if there is a God who created everything, and Jesus is the only way to have a relationship with Him, then who is Jesus? According to the first chapter of the Gospel of John, Jesus is the very Word of God that has become human. To me, it's one of the best descriptions of who Jesus is. It's a longer section of Scripture, so take your time. Ask God to open up your understanding of His Word as you read.

> *In the beginning the Word already existed. The Word was with God, and the Word was God. God created everything through him, and nothing was created except through him. The Word gave life to everything that was created, and his life brought light to everyone. The light shines in the darkness, and the darkness can never extinguish it.*
>
> *God sent a man, John the Baptist, to tell about the light so that everyone might believe because of his testimony. John himself was not the light;*

> *he was simply a witness to tell about the light. The one who is the true light, who gives light to everyone, was coming into the world.*
>
> *He came into the very world he created, but the world didn't recognize him. He came to his own people, and even they rejected him. But to all who believed him and accepted him, he gave the right to become children of God. They are reborn—not with a physical birth resulting from human passion or plan, but a birth that comes from God.*
>
> *So the Word became human and made his home among us. He was full of unfailing love and faithfulness. And we have seen his glory, the glory of the Father's one and only Son.*
>
> *John testified about him when he shouted to the crowds, "This is the one I was talking about when I said, 'Someone is coming after me who is far greater than I am, for he existed long before me.'"*
>
> *From his abundance we have all received one gracious blessing after another. For the law was given through Moses, but God's unfailing love and faithfulness came through Jesus Christ. No one has ever seen God. But the unique One, who is himself God, is near to the Father's heart. He has revealed God to us.*
>
> —John 1:1-18

Jesus was God made flesh—fully man and fully God. The very word of God that was spoken over creation. He came as one of us to show us how to live in relationship with God the Father and to provide a way for us to be saved so we can have that relationship with God. In his book *Mere Christianity*, C. S. Lewis does a great job of explaining the claims Jesus made as God.[13] He says that Jesus would go around telling people their sins were forgiven and how that would only make sense if Jesus truly was the God who was sinned against and whose law was broken. If we take Jesus at His word, then He's either a lunatic, raving about crazy things; a liar and deceiver like the devil; or Lord of all creation. Lewis tried to keep people from claiming that Jesus was a great man with great teachings because it was obvious Jesus did not intend to leave that option open for us.

If we accept Jesus as the sinless Son of God, and if the wages of sin is death, then why did Jesus have to die if He never sinned? The incredible answer is that Jesus died in our place because of *our* sin. He then rose from the dead, defeating death and giving new life to all who would believe in Him. Jesus, then, is God, so we must listen to and take to heart everything He has to say to us.

HOW DO I PLACE MY FAITH IN JESUS?

Jesus's first statement at the beginning of His ministry was, "Repent of your sins and turn to God, for the Kingdom of Heaven is near" (Matthew 4:17b). *Repent* simply means turning away from your sins and toward God, confessing those sins to Him in genuine humility—running away from evil and running toward the goodness of God. As we pursue God, we are to trust Him like a child should be able to trust their parents. A child trusts their parents for everything. If they need anything, they know who to come to, and through that relationship they're able to thrive. That's how we are to be with our Heavenly Father.

I know a lot of people struggle with looking to God as their Father, but that is one of the many ways the Bible

13. C. S. Lewis, *Mere Christianity*, rev. ed. (New York: Macmillan, 1952).

describes Him—as a perfect Heavenly Father. Jesus called the Father *Abba*, which is another word for Father that describes a close and personal relationship. It's one of the first words a Jewish baby would've spoken. A similar term in our language today would be *daddy* or *papa*. If you had a bad father, your Father in heaven wants to show you what a good Father is. If you had a good father, God wants you to trust Him as your Perfect Father.

Will you let Him Father you? This is a question only you can answer, but you must answer it. He is for you and not against you.

> *If God is for us, who can ever be against us? Since he did not spare even his own Son but gave him up for us all, won't he also give us everything else?*
>
> —Romans 8:31b-32

If we feel like He is against us, that is a lie we need to address. Sin and Satan love to try and turn us against God. There are so many lies we believe, but the truth is as Jesus says:

> *For this is how God loved the world: He gave his one and only Son, so that everyone who believes in him will not perish but have eternal life. God sent his Son into the world not to judge the world, but to save the world through him.*
>
> —John 3:16-17

This is a love we can never truly comprehend on this side of heaven, but it is a love that will do whatever it takes to save us. God didn't even keep His only Son from us. He loves us more than we can ever imagine.

Let me say it again for those in the back. God loves you! The Creator of everything loves you! Pause and let that truth sink in. Sin and death could not keep Him from us.

His love is woven throughout all of Scripture and is fully revealed through Jesus Christ. If we would just turn and look to Jesus for the salvation of our souls, we would experience the Father's faithful and unfailing love for us.

Jesus loved keeping it simple:

> *One of them, an expert in religious law, tried to trap him with this question: "Teacher, which is the most important commandment in the law of Moses?" Jesus replied, "'You must love the Lord your God with all your heart, all your soul, and all your mind.' This is the first and greatest commandment. A second is equally important: 'Love your neighbor as yourself.' The entire law and all the demands of the prophets are based on these two commandments."*
>
> —Matthew 22:35-40

Or as I like to say, "Love God and love others."

Did you catch what Jesus said, though? Everything God requires of you is based on those two commandments. Everything in our lives flows from loving God and loving other people. If we have placed our faith in Jesus, then this is what God requires of us.

I've heard it said that placing your faith in something is knowing you can "put your weight on it." Kind of like the partner you trust on shift. The one you know will have your back no matter what. Or placing your faith in a seatbelt to save your life. You're trusting it will help you when you need it.

I definitely experienced the importance of a seatbelt when I had a bad wreck on patrol one night. We received a call about a fight in progress, with knives as the weapon. It was my area, so I was dispatched, along with other officers. I was rolling along pretty well with my lights and siren on, approaching a three-way intersection. I didn't have a stop sign and had the right of way, but the lady turning left in front of me apparently wasn't paying attention. It happened so fast, I just immediately reacted and jerked the steering wheel to the right and ran off the road at a high speed. As soon as I did, I hit my brakes, but the grass was soaked with dew, and it didn't slow me down at all before I centered a large tree just off the roadway. I remember the force of the stop was extremely hard and sudden, knocking the breath out of me. The airbag shot out. It was my first bad wreck like that, so I thought the car was on fire because of the smell from the airbag. I quickly unbuckled and rolled out of the car, and as soon as I could, I radioed for help. My good friend on shift said he could tell it was bad from the sound of my voice over the radio. It completely destroyed the front of my car, but I only sustained minor injuries (cuts, bruises, and a sprained wrist). I attributed this mainly to the seatbelt but also my vest I had on, which likely protected me as well. I know now that God was with me.

This is a good spot to plug a great program for law enforcement called Below 100. Their mission, according to their website, is to stop law enforcement deaths and serious injuries that can be prevented while on duty. They try to do this by focusing on simple and common-sense actions an officer can take to keep themselves safe.[14] Some common sense areas they focus on are wearing your seatbelt, wearing your ballistic vest, and watching your speed. The number of lives that could be saved if law enforcement did those simple things is more than you would think. I wasn't able to watch my speed as well in my situation because I was going to a call that necessitated a rapid response; however, I did have my seatbelt and vest on. I truly believe God used that to save my life that night.

14. "Home," *Below 100*, accessed 2025, https://www.below100.org/

Another God moment in that story is the place where I ran off the road was right next to a large apartment complex. If I had not hit that tree, I could have plowed right through an apartment with a sleeping family inside. There are so many times where I have seen God's protection over me, other fellow first responders, and the public in general. He is a good, good Father.

I'm really grateful for the help the fire department and the ambulance service gave me that night as well. I was pretty shook up, and they took great care of me. Also, the lady that turned in front of me did stop to make sure I was all right and waited until she was released from the scene. Someone told me that after the fact, but I was always grateful for her concern as well.

I placed my faith in that seatbelt, believing that it would help save me in the event of a wreck like that. My faith was rewarded with only minor injuries instead of something worse.

Another great example I've heard used is to imagine yourself on an airplane, standing at the edge of the door waiting to jump. Your plan is that you're going to jump and flap your arms hard enough to try and save yourself. The pilot looks at you like you've lost your mind and throws you a parachute, urging you to trust in it to get down to the ground safely. Jesus is like that parachute or the seatbelt. Our plan to save ourselves and trust in some vague idea that maybe my good outweighs my bad is not going to work. It just ends in death. Put on the Lord Jesus Christ, and let Him save you![15]

Faith is what is required to please God.

---

15. *Living Waters: Inspiring and Equipping Christians,* Living Waters, accessed 2025, https://www.livingwaters.com/. I'd like to acknowledge Ray Comfort and the Living Waters ministry. Some of the information in Chapters 2 and 3 from this book is from the way he shares the Good News of Jesus with people. I think they do an excellent job of clearly presenting the gospel message in a loving way. If you're interested in checking out his ministry, visit their website: https://livingwaters.com/.

> *And Abram believed the Lord, and the Lord counted him as righteous because of his faith.*
> —Genesis 15:6

> *And it is impossible to please God without faith. Anyone who wants to come to him must believe that God exists and that he rewards those who sincerely seek him.*
> —Hebrews 11:6

We should put faith in Jesus like I put faith in that seatbelt, believing that the work He did on the cross is enough to save us from our sins. Turn from sin and look to Him, the risen Lord who defeated death. The Good News about Jesus really is that simple.

THE HELPER

When we put our full weight of faith in Jesus, God the Father sends the Holy Spirit inside us to make us alive in Christ and be our ride or die partner in this life.

> *"But when the Father sends the Advocate as my representative—that is, the Holy Spirit—he will teach you everything and will remind you of everything I have told you."*
> —John 14:26

> *But you are not controlled by your sinful nature. You are controlled by the Spirit if you have the Spirit of God living in you.*
> —Romans 8:9

> *You will receive power when the Holy Spirit comes upon you.*
> —Acts 1:8a

Once we come to faith in Jesus, we are spiritually reborn and able to rely on the Holy Spirit—we now have a new identity with the Father, and we belong to Him. We don't belong to this world, so it can't dictate our worth. We come to know we are sinful and have rebelled against our Father. We trust Jesus and have faith in His work on the cross and His resurrection to save us. We experience His love and forgiveness. Then, He calls us to follow Him.

Here is how Paul describes the Holy Spirit:

> *And Christ lives within you, so even though your body will die because of sin, the Spirit gives you life because you have been made right with God. The Spirit of God, who raised Jesus from the dead, lives in you. And just as God raised Christ Jesus from the dead, he will give life to your mortal bodies by this same Spirit living within you.*
>
> —Romans 8:10-11

As Christ followers, our Father has sent the Spirit of Jesus to live within us, and it is the same power that raised Jesus from the dead. That truth should make our jaws drop open with amazement. The Holy Spirit is life within us! He is how we have power over the sin in our lives. Romans 8 is my favorite chapter in the Bible. The first part of it really talks about the Spirit's power in our life as a follower of Jesus. It talks about how,

- there's no condemnation because the Spirit has freed us from sin (verses 1–2),
- we can be controlled by the Spirit instead of being dominated by sin (verses 5, 9),
- letting the Spirit control our mind leads to life and peace (who doesn't want more of that?) (verse 6),

- even though we will die, the Spirit will give us life because we have been made right with God through Jesus (verse 10),
- like the verse above says, as followers of Jesus, the same Spirit that raised Jesus from the dead lives in us (verse 11),
- we don't have to do what our sinful nature urges us to do; through the power of the Spirit, we can put to death the deeds of our sinful nature and live (verses 12-13),
- if we are led by the Spirit of God, we are children of God (verse 14),
- we haven't received a spirit that makes us fearful, but we received the Spirit when God adopted us as His own children; we can now call God Abba, Father (similar to Daddy or Papa) now (verse 15), and
- His Spirit has joined with ours to affirm that we are God's children (verse 16).

The truth and power of God's words and works are so amazing.

> *By his divine power, God has given us everything we need for living a godly life. We have received all of this by coming to know him, the one who called us to himself by means of his marvelous glory and excellence.*
>
> —2 Peter 1:3

God has given us everything we need, but that doesn't mean following Jesus is going to be easy.

QUESTIONS

- What is Jesus to me? Is He a lunatic, a liar, or the Lord?

- Is Jesus really the Lord of my life, or is something holding me back from trusting Him?

- Do I truly know that God loves me?

- Am I ready to turn to Jesus and follow Him?

PRAYER

God, I have so much to be thankful for, regardless of my circumstances. You have loved me enough to send Jesus to take my place so I can be with You. Thank You! Help me humbly come and surrender my life to You in faith so I can experience Your amazing love for me. In Jesus's name and by the power of the Holy Spirit, Amen.

Chapter 4

SIMPLE BUT NOT EASY

Then Jesus said to his disciples, "If any of you wants to be my follower, you must give up your own way, take up your cross, and follow me. If you try to hang on to your life, you will lose it. But if you give up your life for my sake, you will save it. And what do you benefit if you gain the whole world but lose your own soul? Is anything worth more than your soul?"

—MATTHEW 16:24-26

I love the story in the Gospels about Jesus calming the storm (Matthew 8:23-27, Mark 4:35-41, and Luke 8:22-25). Jesus told His disciples they were going to sail across to the other side of the lake, and then He "settled down for a nap" (Luke 8:23). A strong storm erupted out of nowhere, and in the Gospel of Mark, Mark said the waves were coming into the boat, causing it to fill up with water. The disciples finally decided to shake Jesus awake, asking if He even cared if they drowned. Jesus got up and told the storm to stop—and it did. (Yep! That happened.) Then, Jesus asked them where their faith was.

If you look at the beginning of the story in the Gospels of Mark and Luke, Jesus said to them,

> *"Let's cross to the other side of the lake."*
> —MARK 4:35; LUKE 8:22

When Jesus asked them, "Where is your faith?" in Luke 8:25, He was essentially asking them if they were questioning His ability to keep them safe. I could see Him saying, "Guys, I said we were going to the other side of the lake. You don't trust Me to get you there?" Not to mention He was so at peace that He was fast asleep on a wet boat in the middle of a raging storm. How is that even possible?

I think in His humanity, Jesus was really tired, and He trusted His friends to sail the boat. But I also think it's because He had full faith and trust in God to get them where they were going safely. He knew He was safe in the Father's hands. Whether He died in that boat or not, God the Father was good, and He was one with Him. The freedom He had in relationship with the Father is something we should all desire. He showed us in His life how we should live as children of God. Through faith in Jesus and the power of the Holy Spirit, we can begin to learn to live with that kind of faith too.

Following Jesus is a lifelong process, and He is faithful to see us through. Our loving Father wants to make us more and more like Jesus, even if He has to walk with us through some storms in this life. Just like gold has to be refined by fire for it to be in its purest form, God uses the fires of this life to mold us into the likeness of His Son, Jesus. This process is not easy or comfortable, but it is necessary and will be worth it.

> *I have learned to kiss the waves that throw me up against the Rock of Ages.*
> —Often attributed to Charles H. Spurgeon[16]

After Jesus calms the storm, the Bible says the disciples were absolutely "terrified and amazed" (Luke 8:25). They were initially scared of dying, but now they are awestruck and began asking, "Who is this man?" (Mark 4:41). They thought they knew who Jesus was, but they realized quickly He was much more than they imagined. When the Bible refers to the fear of God, this is what it's talking about: a realization of who you are before God, awestruck and reverent before the Creator of everything.

> *Fear of the Lord is the foundation of wisdom. Knowledge of the Holy One results in good judgement.*
> —Proverbs 9:10

The realization that we have sinned against a holy God should make us feel like Isaiah when he had a vision and saw the Lord.

> *Then I said, "It's all over! I am doomed, for I am a sinful man. I have filthy lips, and I live among a people with filthy lips. Yet I have seen the King, the Lord of Heaven's Armies."*
> —Isaiah 6:5

If we let it, that fear will lead us to faith.

16. While this quote is often attributed to Charles Spurgeon, The Spurgeon Library has said he did not say these exact words. The sentiment behind the quote is consistent with his teachings and is similar to a quote in his 1874 sermon "Sin and Grace," where he said, "The wave of temptation may even wash you higher up upon the Rock of ages, so that you cling to it with a firmer grip than you have ever done before." Used with permission.

TRUSTING THROUGH TRIALS

The disciples learned a valuable lesson about trusting Jesus through the storm. But I wonder if they would have learned the same lesson had it not been for the tough and trying time *through* the storm? I don't think they would have.

As a first responder, it's likely easy to make the decision to serve your community in this way. You decided this would be a rewarding profession and were excited about the possibilities. Then came training or some academy, and you got put through the wringer. Things were suddenly more difficult than you thought they would be. You buckled down, though, and pressed through, finally getting certified in your chosen profession. You were excited that you would finally be able to make a difference! You realized quickly, however, how hard the job can be in so many ways, albeit fulfilling.

An accident scene is a situation where several different first responders come together to serve the public in various capacities: fire, police, dispatch, emergency medical services (EMS), and so on. Depending on how bad the accident is or what's going on, each first responder serves in a different way—but each one is there to help. The scenes can be chaotic, hot, cold, or storming, and it can often be traumatic if there is a severe injury or death involved. It's a time when all our different skills as first responders are put into action, and we focus on doing the best job we can for the people involved. By the time we finish at the scene, we have navigated through the tough circumstances and hopefully helped people manage the traumatic event in the best way possible. These types of calls are not easy, but the way we work as a team in our commitment to public service can still be fulfilling.

This relates to what following Jesus can be like. We make a decision to turn from sin and follow Jesus, only to realize no one told us it was going to be as hard as it is. In fact, it's often extremely difficult! However, if we trust Jesus and find other brothers and sisters in Christ to journey on with, the life of faith is incredibly purposeful and fulfilling.

After the salvation experience, Christians sometimes believe that life is going to be easier for them. I will admit, I am one of these people, and I believed this for a long time. But the more I study God's Word, the more I realize that Jesus never said it would be easy. He did, however, promise to be in it with you, to help you through it, and that it would be worth it in the end.

> *Do not be afraid or discouraged, for the* LORD *will personally go ahead of you. He will be with you; he will neither fail you nor abandon you.*
> —DEUTERONOMY 31:8

> *"And be sure of this: I am with you always, even to the end of the age."*
> —MATTHEW 28:20B

> *For I consider that the sufferings of this present time are not worth comparing with the glory that is to be revealed to us.*
> —ROMANS 8:18 ESV

If you are a child of God, then He is with you through everything this life throws at you. All I've done for Jesus, no matter how hard or seemingly insignificant, has been worthwhile. The purposes of God in the life of a believer are the purposes in life everyone is searching for.

There is a saying in my church: God calls us to "Learn from Christ. Live in Christ. Lead others to Christ." Sure, it sounds easy, but have you ever tried to actually live out the command to love God and love others? To talk to God and read His Word because you want to hear from Him? To love your spouse sacrificially even when you don't feel like it? To be patient with your kids or a coworker? To pray for your enemies and bless them? It's completely opposite to what our human nature is inclined to. When you really try to follow Jesus, it can sometimes feel like all hell comes against you.

That's because it often does.

Thankfully, our peace doesn't come from the world. It comes from Jesus.

> *"I have told you all this so that you may have peace in me. Here on earth you will have many trials and sorrows. But take heart, because I have overcome the world."*
>
> —John 16:33

Jesus doesn't mince words, and you know where you stand with Him. He tells us straight up that we will have trials, sorrows, and difficulties in this life, but we must trust Him through all the storms of life. If we follow Him, He has given us the power we need to push through and overcome the gates of hell.

Many parts of your life will very well get harder after you start following Jesus, especially if you've experienced any kind of trauma and developed some bad coping mechanisms. The Spirit's power is so much greater than anything else, but it can be hard for us to shake off those habits and rely on the Spirit to lead us through our trials. I like how C. S. Lewis addresses this in his *Chronicles of Narnia* book, *The Silver Chair*. (Spoiler alert: the main characters finally locate Prince Rilian, the king's son, who had been imprisoned and brainwashed for years by the evil Queen of Underland. She discovers him freed by the protagonists and speaks to him about what has happened.) The queen raises many questions about why the prince is no longer bound and who the strangers with him are, implying that he was safer while imprisoned. Because he has been captive for so long, the prince initially struggles to break free from the effects of the evil queen's enchantment. In the same way, Lewis suggests that we, too, may find it difficult at first to overcome the sin that has held us captive for so many years.[17]

The lie of the devil is that we were safe where he had us. It's a familiar and comfortable place of death. When we start to shake things up, that's when life can get difficult.

THE REWARDS OF FAITH

I love the mountains. The challenge of the hikes, the amazing views at the top, the connection with nature—all of which I experienced and enjoyed as a child on summer vacations with my family. The challenge of hiking up a mountain trail really reminds me of the truth about how following Jesus can be difficult but completely worthwhile. There's a specific hike that comes to mind in the beautiful Grand Teton mountain range. These mountains were mentioned in John Eldredge's book *Wild at Heart*, which was such a transforming book for me to read during the time when God was doing a major work in my life. Because the book was so impactful for me, I had to go see these mountains for myself!

I was fortunate enough to have this opportunity, along with my dad and brother, as we took a guys adventure to Wyoming. It was a fortieth birthday trip of sorts for me, and our wives were gracious enough to let us go be mountain men for a week. We stayed at a small hotel just north of Jackson Hole, Wyoming, and our trip was planned out to take in some great views and experience some of the local wildlife.

Our longest and most strenuous hike was going to be the Paintbrush Canyon Trail, which began at String Lake at an elevation of 6,800 feet. We had planned to end our hike around Holly Lake, which seemed like a good place to finish our day hike so we could make it back before sundown. We got an early start, getting to see the sun rise and light up the

17. C. S. Lewis, *The Silver Chair* (London: Geoffrey Bles, 1953).

mountains with a beautiful shade of orange. As we trekked through the canyon, we enjoyed the wildlife, the river flowing close to the trail, and the mountains rising up on either side of us. The views on this trail were spectacular and could really take your breath away. God's creation truly is amazing!

On the way up, we got some incredible views of the valley below us, including Leigh Lake and Jackson Lake. It didn't feel like we were rushing, but we still made good time getting to Holly Lake (elevation 9,416 feet) where we had planned to turn around. As we were resting and snacking near the trail, a father hiking with his daughter passed by us. We asked them where they were headed for the day. They were on their way to the summit "not too far" up the trail. We regrouped, deciding the summit was too enticing to turn down. How bad could it be, right?

Well, that "not too far" turned into another 1.8 miles and just over 1,300 more feet in elevation. The uphill hike at that elevation was brutal for us southern guys. Breathing was difficult, and our legs were like jelly, but we were bound and determined to finish. My dad was sixty-six years old at the time, and he was unstoppable. Forging ahead, we had one goal in mind.

Get to the top.

Our progress surely slowed the closer we got to the summit, but we didn't give up. Upon finally reaching the top, we had an emotional moment together where we huddled up and thanked God for the strength to get there. The views from the top, at an elevation of 10,720 feet, were spectacular—made even better by the collective struggle to get there. We enjoyed every minute of our mountaintop experience.

This is an apt analogy to the life of faith. It's much easier, initially, to follow what our selfish nature and this world wants us to do. As soon as you turn around and start following Jesus, you will be traveling a narrow path up the mountain of faith, going against the ways of the world. It will be hard, but those who follow Jesus have a firm foundation to build their lives on that can withstand anything this world throws at them.

I often think of that hike up Paintbrush Canyon Trail with gratitude. We could have taken an easy stroll or slow ride to experience the view of the mountains. That would have been just fine. However, we didn't sign up for *just fine.* We decided to take the hard road and were rewarded with an unforgettable experience. So many people miss out on the adventurous joys of a relationship with Jesus because they're too scared, comfortable, or whatever else. Anything truly good is worth fighting for.

> *I focus on this one thing: Forgetting the past and looking forward to what lies ahead, I press on to reach the end of the race and receive the heavenly prize for which God, through Christ Jesus, is calling us.*
>
> —Philippians 3:13b-14

Jesus also had a straightforward analogy about His teachings:

> *"Anyone who listens to my teaching and follows it is wise, like a person who builds a house on solid rock. Though the rain comes in torrents and the floodwaters rise and the winds beat against that house, it won't collapse because it is built on bedrock. But anyone who hears my teaching and doesn't obey it is foolish, like a person who builds a house on sand. When the rains and floods come and the winds beat against that house, it will collapse with a mighty crash."*
>
> —Matthew 7:24-27

Jesus promises that if you focus on Him, taking the time to build your life on the solid foundation of His life and teachings, then you will not be destroyed, even through the floods and fires of life. But Jesus also issues a warning. If you don't hear and obey His teachings, then your life will "collapse with a mighty crash."

I know Jesus's teachings on this are true because my life is an example of them. My life crashed spectacularly, and I didn't think I would be able to rebuild it. Thanks to God, He had different plans. I now know that a life built on Jesus can withstand any storm, but it can be hard to believe when going through those storms.

Salvation, for me, was bittersweet. I was so incredibly grateful God had saved me, and I couldn't get enough of this new life in Jesus. However, like I mentioned earlier, this was also a tough time for my wife because of my confessions to her about my own sins and struggles. I had deeply hurt and betrayed her with my lies and secrets, and I was unsure if our marriage was going to survive. We had some work to do, and it wasn't going to be easy. It seemed impossible, "but with God all things are possible" (Matthew 19:26b ESV). In time, the Holy Spirit helped us see we were putting each other and other things before God.

My pastor has used a relationship triangle analogy. God is at the top of the triangle, and the husband and wife are opposite each other at the bottom corners. The closer we both individually move toward God, the closer we naturally become with each other. This was very eye opening for us, and we found it to be true the more we followed Jesus. God has since walked us through some extremely difficult life circumstances, including being unable to have biological children. He blessed us beyond our comprehension with two children through the miracle of adoption. God has been with us through my wife's cancer diagnosis as well as on the other side where healing was given. My wife is an amazing and strong woman of God. She does so much for our family, and I honestly don't know where I would be or what I would do without her. I am so grateful for her and see her as a blessing from my Heavenly Father.

God has worked through our pain and has blessed our marriage in so many ways. We've been married for over twenty years now, and it's certainly not because of how good we are but how great our God is. It hasn't been easy, but it has been incredibly fulfilling.

That's how faith is. It isn't easy, but it's worth it.

This is how we should live our lives—steadily pursuing God. As we walk with Him, we will become better in all our relationships. One thing I make sure to always tell my kids is no matter what happens in this life, God is good, and He is with us.

Ever since I turned to Jesus and started following him, my professional career as a first responder has been so much more purposeful and fulfilling. I was able to look at my job with new eyes and see it as a ministry—serving my fellow first responders as well as the public. Again, it hasn't been easy, and I haven't always gotten it right, but that hasn't changed God's purpose for my life. I am here to love God and love other people.

Jesus reminded and counseled us, before following Him, to not "begin until you count the cost" (Luke 14:28a). He wants us to truly think about what we're doing. Are you really ready and willing to die to yourself and live only for Jesus? To suffer alongside Jesus in this world of sin and evil? Only you can make that decision, and there is sacrifice involved. But, spoiler alert: it's worth it.

QUESTIONS

- Like me, did you have a false assumption that life would be easier after following Jesus?

- Does it help to know the truth about what life with Jesus looks like?

- Am I willing to take an honest look at faith in Jesus to see if I am willing to give up my old life for Him?

PRAYER

Jesus, You have made a way for me to be able to experience a relationship with the Heavenly Father. Help me to trust You in this life, even when nothing makes sense. Help me to know that no matter what I am going through, You are good, and You are with me. I love You. Help me know how much You love me. I humbly ask for this in Your mighty name and by the power of the Holy Spirit. Amen.

Chapter 5

BOLO: SPIRITUAL SURVIVAL INSTINCTS

Seek the Lord and his strength; seek his presence continually!

—1 CHRONICLES 16:11 ESV

I hope by now you've felt or heard God encouraging you to know Him in a deeper way. If you feel something stirring in your heart, don't ignore it. God is pursuing you, and He is right there with you. Talk to Him like you would a trusted friend or family member.

The life of faith is absolutely critical to surviving this life and the job of a first responder. Due to its importance, I want to shed some light on things we need to be on the lookout (BOLO) for—some spiritual survival instincts we can hone, by the power of the Holy Spirit, to use for our good and the good of others. These are ways our faith responds when the world is trying to kill us.

Before we get into it, I want to discuss briefly the concept of sanctification. It's a "church" word, but, put simply, sanctification is the steady, persistent, and consistent work of the Holy Spirit in your life to make you more and more like Jesus. It's a process we take part in, and it is the heartbeat of the Christian's walk.

A. W. Tozer makes a great connection regarding this when he talks about the great saints or Christian mystics of the past having "spiritual receptivity." When considering the spiritual greats, like Moses, Elijah, Isaiah, Daniel, Peter, John, and so on, he defines spiritual receptivity in this way:

> *They had spiritual awareness and . . . they went on to cultivate it until it became the biggest thing in their lives.*

He goes on to further explain his position. This book was published in 1948, but the insight into our modern day is amazing to me:

> *The idea of cultivation and exercise, so dear to the saints of old, has now no place in our total religious picture. It is too slow, too common. We now demand glamour and fast-flowing dramatic action. A generation of Christians reared among push buttons and automatic machines is impatient with slower and less-direct methods of reaching their goals. We have been trying to apply machine-age methods to*

> *our relationships with God. . . . These and such as these are the symptoms of an evil disease, a deep and serious malady of the soul.*
> —A. W. Tozer, *The Pursuit of God*[18]

Tozer was on to something, and his words are screaming at our current culture. We are so accustomed, especially in the West, to just having things whenever we want them. We have fast food, fast Wi-Fi, fast cars, etc. It reminds me of that JG Wentworth commercial where all the different people are screaming about their money and how they need it now![19] If we're not careful, we can begin to think this is what our relationship with God should be like. But God's timing and His ways are not like the world's.

> *"At the right time, I, the LORD, will make it happen."*
> —ISAIAH 60:22B

> *"My thoughts are nothing like your thoughts," says the Lord. "And my ways are far beyond anything you could imagine. For just as the heavens are higher than the earth, so my ways are higher than your ways and my thoughts higher than your thoughts."*
> —ISAIAH 55:8-9

In fact, God's ways are totally opposite of the world's ways.

> *"So those who are last now will be first then, and those who are first will be last."*
> —MATTHEW 20:16

---

18. A. W. Tozer, *The Pursuit of God* (Harrisburg, PA: Christian Publications, 1948). Used with permission.

19. JG Wentworth, "It's Your Money," advertisement, YouTube, April 2010, https://m.youtube.com/watch?v=7jY_ZP6gQiQ

What if God is using things in your life for a reason—to develop you spiritually in ways you don't understand and can't see yet? Tozer's insights into exercising and cultivating our faith or "spiritual receptivity" is a great example of sanctification, or the work of the Holy Spirit in our lives. With this idea of being receptive to spiritual realities, let's look at some spiritual survival instincts or disciplines we can develop in our lives to help us follow Jesus.

SELF-CONTROL

> *A person without self-control is like a city with broken-down walls.*
>
> —Proverbs 25:28

Inherent in all spiritual disciplines is the goal of self-control—controlling your body in a way that honors God and is useful for His Kingdom. When we think of discipline, we tend to just think of it negatively, but, as you will see from the examples I'm going to give, disciplining yourself in certain ways can lead to incredible spiritual blessing. Learning how to control yourself begins with controlling your tongue—what you say or don't say. It may seem like an unusual place to start, but James 3:2b says, "For if we could control our tongues, we would be perfect and could also control ourselves in every other way." This seems like the natural starting point for us.

We all know that we should watch what we say and do, but actually following through with that can feel impossible. James goes on to compare the tongue to a small bit in a large horse's mouth, a small rudder on a large ship, and a tiny spark that sets a great forest on fire. The tongue is very small, but it can do so much—for good or for evil.

> *Sometimes it praises our Lord and Father, and sometimes it curses those who have been made in the image of God. And so blessing and cursing come pouring out of the same mouth. Surely, my brothers and sisters, this is not right!*
>
> —James 3:9-10

Jesus said that what we say is an indication of our heart's condition.

> *"A good person produces good things from the treasury of a good heart, and an evil person produces evil things from the treasury of an evil heart.* What you say flows from what is in your heart."
>
> —Luke 6:45, emphasis added

Self-control includes bringing not only your tongue but your entire body under control by the power of the Holy Spirit to make it do what you know God wants you to do. It's not being at the beck and call of our physical bodies but striving to follow the Spirit's leading in every area of our lives.

At one time in a community where I worked, there was a man who we always compared to Otis from *The Andy Griffith Show*—the town drunk who was always in and out of jail. (I'll just call him Otis for the purpose of this illustration.) Otis came before the municipal judge for court one day on some small misdemeanor charge, and the judge sentenced him to pay a fine. He said, "Judge, you know I can't pay that. Can I do something else to pay for it? Like jumping jacks or something?" Even the judge laughed at that one.

Late one night on shift, I had a small but memorable encounter with Otis. Several officers and I were out working a safety checkpoint when we saw him walking toward us.

Otis had his signature strut going on, and we could tell he had already gone through several *beverages*. Before we could even say anything, Otis started singing "Bad Boys," the opening theme song from the television show *Cops*.[20] When he finished, he looked at us and said, "Y'all know I wrote that song, right?" Otis didn't give us a chance to answer and just started cackling at his own joke, very pleased with himself. We smiled and shook our heads. Just another night on shift.

Otis is a prime example of someone not having self-control when it comes to drinking. Before you point fingers, though, think about areas in your life where you don't have great self-control. Can you control your anger? How about your online activities? Can you stop drinking before you become drunk, or do you have to drink excessively to have a good time? What about gossip? Do you just have to join the conversation? Those pills the doctor prescribed; can you stop taking them, or are you trying to get more? While these examples certainly aren't exhaustive, they can help you start thinking about areas in your life where you could exercise more self-control. I have to constantly reevaluate where I am with self-control as well, so it is a daily surrendering to the Spirit's conviction and leading.

Paul goes through a similar list of desires that comes from our sinful nature:

> *When you follow the desires of your sinful nature, the results are very clear: sexual immorality, impurity, lustful pleasures, idolatry, sorcery, hostility, quarreling, jealousy, outbursts of anger, selfish ambition, dissension, division,*

20. I. Lewis, "Bad Boys" (theme from *Cops*), on *Bad Boys (Theme from Cops) – Single*, Sound Bwoy Ent/DubShot Records, 1987.

> *envy, drunkenness, wild parties, and other sins like these.*
>
> —Galatians 5:19-21a

He warns that "anyone living that sort of life will not inherit the Kingdom of God" (Galatians 5:21b) and counters these destructive behaviors with the life-giving characteristics that only the Holy Spirit can develop within us.

> *But the Holy Spirit produces this kind of fruit in our lives: love, joy, peace, patience, kindness, goodness, faithfulness, gentleness, and self-control. There is no law against these things!*
>
> —Galatians 5:22-23

I love these verses and how they contrast each other. Especially when Paul exclaims there is no law against anything that is a product of the Holy Spirit. So we can love as much as we want and won't get in trouble! There's no such thing as too much peace, and the more self-control we have, the better our lives will be. We are free to work on these as much as we want to.

As first responders, we tend to give ourselves a pass when it comes to this kind of stuff. We see ourselves as fighting the good fight of public service. Contributing to the good of humanity and being the backbone of our communities. We can fall into the mindset of agreeing that we're not perfect but that we are way better than the vast majority of the people we deal with. So we should get a pass, right?

Wrong. Those are just excuses for the evil we allow in our lives. God longs for us to surrender fully to His leading because He knows it is ultimately for our good and His glory. So let's press on into some more spiritual disciplines to find, perhaps surprisingly, how they can lead to the freedom of our souls.

FIGHTING COMPLACENCY

> *Fools are destroyed by their own complacency.*
> —Proverbs 1:32

> *Complacency is a deadly foe of all spiritual growth.*
> —A. W. Tozer, *The Pursuit of God*[21]

Once we find our identity through faith in Christ alone, we must fix our eyes on Him and, with the help of the Holy Spirit inside of us, follow Jesus along the narrow way. Keeping it simple, that means we must daily seek to hear from the Father by digging into His Word, the Bible, and talking to Him through prayer. If we make it a daily habit to seek God's Kingdom above all else and live rightly, then He will give us all we need (see Matthew 6:33).

One of the main problems we can all run into in our walk is complacency. Everyone has an idea of what complacency is, and first responders should have a healthy respect for how dangerous it can be. I have certainly experienced it in my spiritual life as well as my professional life. *Complacency* is being really sure of yourself and abilities while, at the same time, unaware of personal weaknesses and present dangers.[22] When we're complacent, we become arrogant and self-satisfied, leaving us vulnerable and open to attack. As we hone our skills through practice and training, we become aware of the potential dangers and our weaknesses and can strive to mitigate those.

21. A. W. Tozer, *The Pursuit of God* (Harrisburg, PA: Christian Publications, 1948). Used with permission.

22. "Complacency," *Merriam-Webster.com Dictionary*, accessed July 25, 2025, https://www.merriam-webster.com/dictionary/complacency

I'll tell on myself with this story, but it's a good example of what complacency looks like. I was working night shift and patrolling the area when I noticed a car going way too fast on one of the backroads in the city. I flipped my lights on and whipped my cruiser around to make the traffic stop. I got the car to stop and walked up to the vehicle, a beat-up old Chevrolet Blazer, and started talking with the occupants. A guy was driving, and there was a female passenger. I could tell something was up just by how nervous they were and how their story of why they were going so fast and where they were coming from didn't add up.

After checking the driver's identification, I saw that he had a warrant, and the passenger didn't have a valid driver's license. I also found some illegal drugs on the driver, so I arrested him and searched the vehicle before having it towed and allowing the passenger to call for a ride. Because I found drugs, I searched the guy before putting him in the back of my cruiser. My backup finished with the stop while I transported the guy to our police department for booking.

We arrived at the booking room and started processing the guy for the arrest. We got to the point where we were going to have to strip search him due to the drugs we found on him; we wanted to make sure he was not hiding drugs in other places. Once he realized we are going to do that, he got really nervous and started shaking. We asked him what was going on, thinking he may have swallowed some of the drugs. He said, "I have a gun on me." My partner and I took control of him and asked him where it was. He told us it was strapped to his chest, which was exactly where we found it. I thought I had searched him thoroughly for weapons and drugs, but I did not check that high on his chest.

I had gotten complacent with my searches.

Thankfully, we were able to secure the gun and complete the booking process without anything bad happening. Afterwards, I was the one shaken up and really upset at myself for putting us all at risk. I had gotten lax on my searching and awareness and didn't even know there was danger close. It is a lesson I will never forget, and I am so thankful someone didn't get hurt because of my complacency. Yet another example of God's protection!

If we have to fight against complacency at work all the time, how much more should we fight against complacency in our spiritual lives? For some reason, this truth flies under the radar, and we put off developing our relationship with God. If we don't take steps to stay close with Jesus every day, then we're not going to be ready when we need to fight against the evil around us. Complacency and distractions, which we'll talk about in the next chapter, work together in this regard. We're complacent and apathetic toward our relationship with Jesus, and we are distracted by the things of the world, considering worldly things more important than God.

How many times have we lost the fight against sin? If you're like me, it's been countless times. Every time we do it's because we have become complacent in our relationship with God. He hasn't changed or gone anywhere. We are the ones who have turned away from Him to worship everything this world offers. The difference in our jobs is we tend to be more aware of the potential dangers of being a first responder, so we try to train and prepare accordingly. The supernatural/spiritual realm, however, is unseen but more dangerous than we realize. The training ground for our fight against complacency in our spiritual walk is knowing the Word of God and praying to our loving Heavenly Father. Yes, I know this is the "church" answer, but if it's the truth, why do we need to try to come up with something else?

The truth stands on its own.

TUNNEL VISION

> *Let us strip off every weight that slows us down, especially the sin that so easily trips us up. And let us run with endurance the race God has set before us. We do this by* keeping our eyes on Jesus, *the champion who initiates and perfects our faith.*
>
> —Hebrews 12:1b-2a, emphasis added

I like this idea of having tunnel vision, where all we see is Jesus and we keep our eyes fixed on Him as we walk through this life. If you're in law enforcement, you've definitely heard the term *tunnel vision* in reference to one of your body's many natural responses in a survival situation. For those who don't know, when you're faced with a life-or-death situation, your body naturally responds in certain ways to help keep you alive. One of those ways is your vision narrows so you can focus on what's in front of you. In law enforcement, it can be a bad thing because you lose situational awareness.

We are taught several techniques to battle this, but it's interesting to me how our body reacts because of the survival instincts that God created us with. When our bodies are hit with a life-or-death situation, they respond in ways meant to help keep us alive. Physically this happens when the body is under stress. Maybe that's why struggles and persecution drive us closer to God. When we're put under spiritual stress, our soul kicks into survival mode, helping us focus more clearly on God.

Question: Could some of the troubles in your life be allowed by God because He knows it's the only way you will fix your eyes on Him?

This is definitely not the only reason for troubles and heartache, but God can use everything to help us stay close to Him. Remember, the goal is to trust Jesus and be more and more like Him. God loves you so much, He will do whatever it takes to get your attention. God loves us, but He also knows what's best for us. The best thing for us is God Himself. Everything else is temporary and fading away, but God is forever.

> *So we don't look at the troubles we can see now; rather, we fix our gaze on things that cannot be seen. For the things we see now will soon be gone, but the things we cannot see will last forever.*
> —2 Corinthians 4:18

The story in the Gospel of Matthew where Peter stepped out of the boat and walked on water is pretty cool. Jesus had instructed the disciples to take the boat and go to the other side of the lake while He stayed back with the crowd of people and then later went to pray. While the disciples were crossing the lake, a strong wind started making heavy waves, and they fought with all their might to not sink. At about 3 o'clock in the morning, they started freaking out because they thought they saw a ghost walking on the water.

> *When the disciples saw him walking on the water, they were terrified. In their fear, they cried out, "It's a ghost!" But Jesus spoke to them at once. "Don't be afraid," he said. "Take courage. I am here!" Then Peter called to him, "Lord, if it's really you, tell me to come to you, walking on the water." "Yes, come," Jesus said. So Peter went over the side of the boat and*

> *walked on the water toward Jesus. But when he saw the strong wind and the waves, he was terrified and began to sink. "Save me, Lord!" he shouted. Jesus immediately reached out and grabbed him. "You have so little faith," Jesus said. "Why did you doubt me?" When they climbed back into the boat, the wind stopped. Then the disciples worshiped him. "You really are the Son of God!" they exclaimed.*
>
> —MATTHEW 14:26-33

We'll talk more about Peter later, but if you know a little about his attitude and personality throughout Scripture, it's not surprising that he would ask Jesus to let him walk on the water. Peter was bold, and he wanted to have bold faith. It may have surprised Peter when Jesus told him to come to Him, but Peter took a step of faith that caused him to do the impossible. He started walking to Jesus on the water!

I imagine Peter was looking at Jesus in amazement, trying to wrap his mind around what was happening. Just a second ago, he was in the boat with his friends, scared of the storm, but, being a fisherman, he was in his element. He knew how to handle the situation to help get them to safety. Once he took that step of faith outside the boat, all bets were off. All he had was Jesus. There was nothing he could do to save himself. The only thing he had to do was keep his eyes fixed on Jesus and trust Him in the midst of the storm.

Instead, Scripture tells us,

> *But when he saw the strong wind and the waves, he was terrified and began to sink. "Save me, Lord!" he shouted.*
>
> —MATTHEW 14:30

Peter took his eyes off Jesus. He focused on the storm instead of the One who could save him *through* the storm.

That's when he began to sink. As soon as he knew he was going down, he locked back onto Jesus and screamed for help, pleading with Jesus to save him. Matthew says in his Gospel that Jesus "immediately reached out and grabbed him" (Matthew 14:31). There was no hesitation from Jesus once Peter asked Him for help. Jesus then rebuked Peter for his lack of faith and for doubting that Jesus would come through for him. He asked Peter (and He asks us), "Why did you doubt me?"

Why do *we* doubt Him?

If Peter had Jesus right there with him and yet still doubted, then how much more so do we need to keep our eyes fixed on Jesus? The wind and waves of this life will drown us unless we look to Jesus and cry out for His help.

FITNESS

> *Physical training is good, but training for godliness is much better, promising benefits in this life and in the life to come.*
>
> —1 Timothy 4:8

Physical exercise is only beneficial if done consistently over time. Committing to an exercise and diet plan takes discipline because the results take time. It's not a quick fix, and it's definitely not easy or comfortable. You can't just work out for one day and be an incredible athlete. There's a Nike commercial I really like that shows a lot of athletes going through various types of strenuous training, really struggling. The end of the advertisement says, "Winning isn't comfortable." If you want to see results physically, you have to put in the work over a consistent period of time; you can't stop. If you have been exercising for a long time, and you get off your routine and miss some days, it doesn't take long to lose the progress you've achieved.

I came across a devotional from Danny Saavedre called *A Workout Plan that Works!* It had some good insight into this truth by comparing fitness with sanctification—how it's the process of getting us in spiritual shape so that we can be used for what God wants to do in our lives. To practice godly habits and spiritual disciplines daily, allowing the Spirit to work within us, making us spiritually healthy.[23]

Physical fitness is a critical part of having a successful career as a first responder and a thriving life afterwards, but it involves more than just *working out.* It also includes diet and sleep. Just like a life of faith is more than just one decision to follow Jesus, we must continue to follow Him every day, utilizing spiritual disciplines—like studying Scripture, prayer, worship, fasting, fellowship, service, generosity, sharing your faith, etc.—to grow stronger in faith by the power of the Holy Spirit. Faith in Jesus is the foundation. We build on that foundation when we train spiritually every day. The more you train, by the help of the Spirit, the easier it gets to know the will of God and the way He wants you to go.

I might as well tell on myself again and get it out of the way. I weighed a lean and mean two hundred pounds out of the police academy. I'm six feet five inches, though, so that wasn't a lot of weight for my frame. Once I graduated from the academy and got on night shift, I wasn't consistent with my physical exercise and neglected my diet. Unfortunately, a healthy diet doesn't include night shift fast food. Before I knew it, I looked at my midsection and noticed it jiggling more than before. I stepped on the scale and thought it had to be wrong—two hundred fifty pounds! I was shocked into doing something about it, so I started eating better and exercising. Now, I've got a solid dad bod going, where you can tell I work out but won't turn down a cheeseburger.

23. D. Saavedre, "A Workout Plan That Works," devotional, YouVersion Bible App, originally released July 10, 2008.

As I've mentioned, faith is the most critical aspect of a healthy and purposeful life as a first responder, but we can't forget to take care of our physical bodies as well. I believe taking care of our bodies is actually a part of walking in faith. God's Word has some things to say about that, like the verse at the beginning of this chapter says—physical training is good. It allows you to do the things the Lord has called you to do for as long as He allows it.

> *Don't you realize that your body is the temple of the Holy Spirit, who lives in you and was given to you by God? You do not belong to yourself, for God bought you with a high price. So you must honor God with your body.*
>
> —1 Corinthians 6:19-20

Paul uses this example in light of sexual sin, but the principle is the same. If you follow Jesus, then the Holy Spirit has been given to you and has taken up residence inside you. So you should honor God with your body because of that. Before Jesus, the presence of God resided in the Temple in Jerusalem. Now, because of what Jesus has done, God is moving into His people and using them to show the world how they can be brought back into relationship with Him. We need to take care of our bodies physically and, even more so, spiritually.

There are interesting stories in the Gospel of John about Jesus proclaiming He offers living water and is the bread of life. The first story is with the Samaritan woman at the well in John chapter 4. Jesus specifically offers this woman living water. She's confused because she's thinking about real water, but Jesus is really talking about faith in Him and what that looks like.

> *Jesus replied, "Anyone who drinks this water will soon become thirsty again. But those who drink*

> *the water I give will never be thirsty again. It becomes a fresh, bubbling spring within them, giving them eternal life."*
>
> —John 4:13-14

A "fresh, bubbling spring within"—who doesn't want that?

In John chapter 6, starting at verse 22 right after Jesus feeds the five thousand, He has a large crowd of people following Him because they know He can provide for their physical needs. Again, the entire interaction Jesus has with the crowd is really interesting and amazing to me, but Jesus says this in verse 35:

> *Jesus replied, "I am the bread of life. Whoever comes to me will never be hungry again. Whoever believes in me will never be thirsty."*
>
> —John 6:35

Jesus makes that connection and relation of sustenance for our physical body to our spiritual hunger. He knows how much our bodies crave food and drink. He's trying to open our eyes to how much our soul is craving life, peace, and joy. He offers it to everyone here, and He's still offering it to everyone now.

Yes, even to you.

> *Jesus stood and shouted to the crowds, "Anyone who is thirsty may come to me! Anyone who believes in me may come and drink! For the Scriptures declare, 'Rivers of living water will flow from his heart.'" (When he said, "living water," he was speaking of the Spirit, who would be given to everyone believing in him.)*
>
> —John 7:37b-39a

We understand the basic disciplines necessary to stay healthy—we need to maintain a decent diet and implement some form of consistent exercise. Jesus says your spiritual life is more important, and the disciplines are similar. Feed off of His life and teachings that will forever sustain us, and keep coming back to Him consistently. It's the exercising of the soul that we need to do each and every day.

Distraction is another major spiritual issue we should BOLO for; however, I'm going to address that in the next chapter because of how important it is. Before we move on, though, use the questions below to consider what we've discussed in this chapter. Satan and our own sins love to tempt and attack us where we're weak. A great first step is knowing your areas of weakness so you can invite God to come be the strength you need to overcome.

QUESTIONS

- What are some areas of weakness I need to BOLO for and ask the Holy Spirit to help me strengthen?

- I'm still not sold on following Jesus. What is holding me back?

- I am a follower of Jesus. Have I become complacent, unfocused, and unfit in my faith?

- What am I going to do about it?

PRAYER

Holy Spirit, I need You. I need You to give me faith and to strengthen that faith. Give me the tools I need to grow deeper in my relationship with You. Help me to use Your gifts to further the Father's Kingdom right now. I can't do this on my own. I want to pursue Jesus with my whole heart. Please help me do this. Amen.

Chapter 6

DISTRACTIONS

Guard your heart above all else, for it determines the course of your life. . . . Don't get sidetracked; keep your feet from following evil.

—Proverbs 4:23, 27

Josiah Queen has a great song called "Dusty Bibles" that my daughter loves.[24] In it he makes the observation that we have brand new phones but our Bibles are sitting around with dust on them. Then we wonder why we struggle in so many ways and feel the way we do. Distractions, like phones can be, are subtle but powerful tools the enemy uses to keep us from a vibrant and fulfilling relationship with our Heavenly Father. They may not seem like a big deal, but they can grow to be a huge stumbling block for our faith—like a small snowball rolling down a hill. Before you know it, it has grown into something you can't stop.

24. J. Queen, J. Howell, Z. Lawson, and D. Thomas, "Dusty Bibles," on *Mt. Zion*, Josiah Queen Music, 2025.

This has been a big step for me to realize just how powerful some distractions are in my life. Obviously there are things in life we inherently know are bad for us. As Christians, by the power of the Holy Spirit, we should root those things out of our lives and not turn back to them. However, there are lots of things in this world that are not inherently bad, but we can still become enslaved to them or idolize them.

> *You say, "I am allowed to do anything"—but not everything is good for you. And even though "I am allowed to do anything," I must not become a slave to anything.*
>
> —1 Corinthians 6:12

Now, I want to be clear. Anything we do to help us get closer to God or to serve God or serve others is meant to be an overflow from the salvation we already have in Jesus. Our good works or actions do not save us. They were never meant to. We've already talked through this, but I must reiterate it because of the tendency we have to depend on ourselves and not on God.

Jesus has done *all* the work to save us, and it is enough.

Period.

Once we are born again through faith in Jesus and the power of the Holy Spirit, we receive the Holy Spirit to help us live like Jesus more and more every day. The new life in Christ brings new desires, passions, thoughts, motives, and so on. If you don't have this new life and these motivations, then it should make you question whether or not you have trusted in Jesus alone for your salvation. Anything we do after being born again is to help us stay close to God, become more and more like Jesus, be productive for His Kingdom, and help us love others with the love of God.

LEVERAGING LENT

If you're a guy or have a son about to hit his teenage years, I highly recommend the book *Play the Man* by Mark Batterson.[25] Even though the book is directed toward men and sons and is great in that regard, one of the principles that resonated with me is universal. The author mentions leveraging the season of Lent before Easter to help clear out distractions, increase your awareness of and dependence on God, and deepen your intimacy with God. If you're not familiar with Lent, it's a forty-day period before Easter, during which Christians typically fast and pray to help strengthen their relationship with God.

I felt a conviction in the area of distractions not long ago regarding social media. For me it wasn't necessarily a bad thing, on the surface. Scrolling through to see what was happening in everyone's lives—it was something to do in my down time. Some of the content was funny and even wholesome. I noticed, however, that it began to cut into my family time. I was a scrolling zombie, absorbed in my phone and not spending time with my family. The Holy Spirit convicted me, and I decided to use the time during Lent to break that habit. I took apps off my phone and stopped using those platforms during that time of Lent.

I really can't overstate the results of this practice for me. I didn't realize how much time I was spending on stuff that really didn't matter. Along with more time with my family, it opened up more time with God through praying and reading the Bible—not to mention reading in general, which I've always enjoyed, time to write and create music, and time to just be still and know that He is God (Psalm 46:10). God even used the time to spur on the idea and possibility for this

25. M. Batterson, *Play the Man: Becoming the Man God Created You to Be* (Grand Rapids, MI: Baker Books, 2018).

book. If I would have stayed distracted, this book wouldn't exist. The power of *small* and *no big deal* distractions was revealed in amazing ways.

How much time do you spend on your phone? Go into your phone settings and see, if you dare.

It'll shock you.

The band Wolves at the Gate have a song called "Synthetic Sun" that speaks to this idea of how technology and screens (phones, computers, tablets, televisions, and so forth) are false lights that can blind us to what is truly real.[26] We use all these things to entertain, inform, and guide, but ultimately they are blinding and killing us from within. It reminds me of Jesus's words at the end of Matthew chapter 6:

> *"Your eye is like a lamp that provides light for your body. When your eye is healthy, your whole body is filled with light. But when your eye is unhealthy, your whole body is filled with darkness. And if the light you think you have is actually darkness, how deep that darkness is!*
> —Matthew 6:22-23

Your eye—that is, the things you look at and honor with your attention—can impact your spiritual health, even blinding you to make you think you are actually living in the light when in reality it's darkness. That's why Jesus said if the light you think you have is actually darkness, then consider how deep that darkness really is. It should profoundly concern us that we could be walking in darkness without even realizing it, thinking that we are walking in the light. We think we're doing OK by making it through life without any major difficulties. We feel like we should spend more

26. S. Cobucci and A. Collingsworth, "Synthetic Sun," on *Wasteland*, Solid State Records, 2025.

time with God, but really we don't have the time, failing to consider the spiritual consequences of not actively pursuing God and abiding in Jesus every day.

Another conviction for me during the next season of Lent was caffeine. I know, I know. It's almost blasphemous to even suggest a caffeine fast, but it was a conviction for me because I felt like I was depending more on it than on God. Again, the step I took to clear out a distraction and fill it in with godly things was used by God to bring us closer. If that sounds like something you might want to try, I would suggest weaning yourself off caffeine prior to the fast or contacting a doctor before you do it, depending on what your caffeine intake is. I went *cold turkey*, and, while I was able to keep it going, some of the effects on my body were unexpected, to say the least.

I'm not telling you these things to brag, but to show you practical things God can use to help your relationship with Him and others grow and heal. If you're having problems with the same type of sins over and over, fasts are great ways to stimulate change. Depriving yourself of certain things helps us realize that what we really need is not more *things* in this life but more of God Himself.

> *Then Jesus was led by the Spirit into the wilderness to be tempted there by the devil. For forty days and forty nights he fasted and became very hungry. During that time the devil came and said to him, "If you are the Son of God, tell these stones to become loaves of bread." But Jesus told him, "No! The Scriptures say, 'People do not live by bread alone, but by every word that comes from the mouth of God.'"*
>
> —Matthew 4:1-4

That's why food fasts can be so effective for us spiritually if we focus on seeking God through prayer and through His Word, connecting our physical hunger to the hunger of our souls for the Great I AM. If we draw near to God in this way, He will draw near to us.

> *Draw near to God, and he will draw near to you.*
>
> —JAMES 4:8A ESV

As I look back on that time now, I see it as a sort of mid-life spiritual revival for me. Better than the alternative mid-life crisis, that's for sure! We need to be praying and yearning for spiritual revival in our lives and the lives of those around us. God blessed these moments where I deprived myself and sought after Him. I really felt during that time like the things this world places value on were fading away. I began longing for heavenly things. I told my brother, the best way I could describe it was I could feel the edges of eternity around me, like God was giving me spiritual senses to feel the unseen supernatural side of life. I attribute it to the fact that God was drawing near to me because I was drawing near to Him. I am so grateful for the work He has done in me. I just want everyone to experience closeness with God. He is there—we just have to pursue Him.

Distractions can come in a variety of forms: television, video games, relationships, sports, music, vehicles, clothing, and so on. Essentially anything that takes you away from God, your family, and what He has called you to do is a distraction. These types of things are what the enemy uses to keep us under control and ineffective for God's Kingdom. I don't think we understand the full impact they have on our daily walk with God.

LESSON LEARNED

I'll share a rookie cop story about my first car chase and foot pursuit that kind of ties into this idea of distraction. I was on night shift, and it was approaching early morning as I continued patrolling and ran across someone speeding. I turned around on them and noticed they sped up once I turned my lights on. I hit my siren, and the chase was on—in my older model Ford Crown Victoria. The vehicle was going really fast, and I was white knuckling the steering wheel as we sped over the rough streets and around the sharp curves. They fled back into the large city that bordered the city of the department I worked for, trying to lose me in a large subdivision notorious for the many roads and similar-sounding street names.

I had no clue where I was.

I finally caught up to the car and saw the driver, a guy, bail out of the car and start running away. I slid to a stop and jumped out to take off after him, actually having the wherewithal to lock my car up. I saw him running through some brush, so I kept him in sight and took off after him.

Now, if you've been a first responder long, you know how hard it is to run in all that gear you're carrying around. It's like your legs all of a sudden don't want to work right!

This suspect was trying to lose me in the thick brush, but I wasn't stopping. I had a barbed wire fence hidden by the thicket catch my leg, cutting me and ripping my pants. I pulled it off me and kept going, fueled by adrenaline. I finally caught up to him and tackled him to the ground. We wrestled for a minute before I was able to get him under control with one hand behind his back. The other hand was tucked tight under his body, and he wasn't giving it up. I let off of him a little to try and get his hand out from under him, but he bucked me off and turned to face me as we both got up. I pulled my handgun and ordered him to stop and put his hands behind his back. (Sidenote: I had some pepper spray with me, but, because of the chaos and inexperience on my part, it never crossed my mind to use it).

As I was standing there, pointing my gun at him and giving him orders, there was an awkward pause as he stared down the barrel of my gun with his hands up before he said, "I ain't got no gun. You can't shoot me." Another awkward pause while I thought about what he just said, then cursed (yeah, remember that *not perfect* part) while I quickly put my gun back in my holster. He took that opportunity to go back to running away. I took off after him again, but the adrenaline was wearing off, and I was completely gassed. Again, if you're a first responder, you understand how quickly your body can wear down after a foot pursuit and fight.

I stopped with my hands on my knees and watched him run off in the distance down the dark, quiet street while I caught my breath with my uniform all messed up, bleeding from my cut, and the lapel mic from my radio dangling by my side. (Equipment never stays on like it should.) Thankfully, backup arrived shortly thereafter. How they found me, I don't know, because I was lost and had not given any updates over the radio after getting out of my car.

I'm grateful for everyone on my shift that night because they really cared about me and helped me out after it was done. They may or may not have given me a little bit of a hard time about it. I was able to positively identify the guy from a photograph so we could sign charges against him; however, I never found out why he ran from me that day.

Many believe that on-the-job training is one of the best ways you can really learn how to do something—and I believe it. You can know all about everything, but when the rubber meets the road and you have to put into practice what you've learned, well, that's a whole other thing.

I learned that I needed to start figuring out how to mitigate the effects adrenaline can have on my body. I was completely focused and tunnel-visioned in on catching that guy, which caused me to forget what tools I had at my disposal and forget to update my location and situation over the radio to my fellow officers who were trying to come help me. I needed to clear out the distractions so I could clearly see what I needed to do. As first responders, training is an important part of what helps us fight through situations like that and make sound decisions in the middle of a chaotic environment.

Our spiritual lives are no different. God doesn't bring us back to life again just to leave us alone. He has given us His Spirit and promises that He is always with us. His Word and prayer are vital areas of training that we have been neglecting. Scripture trains our spiritual ears to hear from God, and prayer builds our spiritual relationship with God. We say we love Jesus but never spend time with Him or seek to know what He requires of us. That's like saying you love your spouse but never spend any time with them. You probably wouldn't be married for long with a relationship like that!

WHAT IS DISTRACTING YOU?

As we're walking along with Jesus in faith, we need to really take a look at our lives and see what areas are prone to turn us away from God, however small they may seem. Then, take practical steps similar to what I've laid out, but whatever the Spirit convicts you of, to change the way you are living out your life.

A couple of good questions to ask yourself are as follows:

- Is Jesus just another part of my life, or is Jesus my entire life?

- Does everything I do stem from my faith and trust in Jesus and the power of the Holy Spirit, or do I seek to live my life under my own power?
- What is keeping me distracted from time with God?

Now, I want to reiterate that I am not perfect. I love how Paul Washer puts it in one of his sermons. He says we don't contribute anything to our salvation but our sin, and nothing to our ministries or lives of faith but our weaknesses. Our only hope is Christ.[27] The Holy Spirit has convicted me of weaknesses in my own life and has given me the power to do something about them. I certainly don't bat one thousand percent with this, but the more I stay connected to God, the more He can work through me. Jesus gave a great example of this when He talked about abiding in Him:

> *"Remain in me, and I will remain in you. For a branch cannot produce fruit if it is severed from the vine, and you cannot be fruitful unless you remain in me. Yes, I am the vine; you are the branches. Those who remain in me, and I in them, will produce much fruit. For apart from me you can do nothing."*
> —John 15:4-5

This has been a recurring theme in my life as I try to humble myself before God every day and remain in Jesus through this life. We are the branch, and Jesus is the Vine. We cannot produce good works (or fruit) for the Kingdom of God unless we remain in Jesus and rely on the power of the Holy Spirit.

> *"A good tree produces good fruit, and a bad tree produces bad fruit. A good tree can't produce*

27. HeartCry Missionary Society, *Part 1: There Is Only One Hero, Freedom in the Gospel, Paul Washer – Mississippi Prison, HeartCry*, YouTube video, January 2025, https://www.youtube.com/watch?v=1isjzqF18tk

bad fruit, and a bad tree can't produce good fruit. So every tree that does not produce good fruit is chopped down and thrown into the fire. Yes, just as you can identify a tree by its fruit, so you can identify people by their actions. Not everyone who calls out to me, 'Lord! Lord!' will enter the Kingdom of Heaven. Only those who actually do the will of my Father in heaven will enter. On judgment day many will say to me, 'Lord! Lord! We prophesied in your name and cast out demons in your name and performed many miracles in your name.' But I will reply, 'I never knew you. Get away from me, you who break God's laws.'"

—MATTHEW 7:17-20

The end of this verse is one of the scariest and most sobering warnings Jesus gave. There will be people who did good things and had the appearance of following Jesus but never trusted in Him to save them. They claimed to know Jesus, but their hearts were far from Him. It will cause them to be separated from Him for eternity. It also reminds me of Jesus's words in Matthew 5:

"So if your eye—even your good eye—causes you to lust, gouge it out and throw it away. It is better for you to lose one part of your body than for your whole body to be thrown into hell. And if your hand—even your stronger hand—causes you to sin, cut it off and throw it away. It is better for you to lose one part of your body than for your whole body to be thrown into hell."

—MATTHEW 5:29-30

If there is something keeping you from Jesus, may God give you the strength to cut it off and throw it out of your life so you can run to Him. Sins, distractions, and even the good things you do are separating you from a personal relationship with Jesus—now *and* in eternity.

I haven't mentioned hell yet, but Jesus talked about it so we need to as well. In the previous verse, Jesus used a graphic analogy to shock us into a realization of what's at stake. He also used a story in Luke to illustrate the afterlife. In Luke 16:19-31, Jesus tells the story of a rich man and a beggar named Lazarus (whose name means "God is my help"). The rich man had everything this world could offer, and Lazarus had nothing—not even physical health, because the dogs would come lick his sores. The rich man had no concern for anyone but himself, but Lazarus, as his name would indicate, had put his faith in God alone. Both men die, and Lazarus goes to heaven while the rich man goes to hell. The rich man was in agony, and Lazarus was being comforted. The roles had been eternally reversed.

This story is a sobering reminder of life from an eternal perspective. This physical life we see is not all there is. Hell is eternal and complete separation from God, and heaven is eternal and complete connection with God. If we put the things of this world before God and don't want to be with Him, then He's going to honor that decision.

Are you going to just sit around and let life's distractions drag you into hell? Don't wait! Look closely at your life and faith to see where your loyalties lie.

> *As God's partners, we beg you not to accept this marvelous gift of God's kindness and then ignore it. For God says, "At just the right time, I heard you. On the day of salvation, I helped you." Indeed, the "right time" is now. Today is the day of salvation.*
>
> —2 Corinthians 6:1-2

> *Remember what it says: "Today when you hear his voice, don't harden your hearts as Israel did when they rebelled."*
>
> —Hebrews 3:15

Again, if there are obvious things in our lives we know are wrong, then, as followers of Jesus, we should immediately ask the Holy Spirit to help us get rid of whatever those things are. Turn from them and turn to Jesus. However, there could be things in your life, as a follower of Jesus, that aren't necessarily *bad* on the surface but are keeping or hindering you from a deeper and more fruitful relationship with Jesus. We need to seek God's help to get rid of those things as well because they could be keeping you from accomplishing the good plans God has for your life.

I'll close this chapter with an excerpt from John Eldredge's book *Experience Jesus. Really.*

> *God longs to bless us, strengthen us, guide us. He truly does. What I want you to notice is found in the last sentence: "For he has rescued us from the dominion of darkness and brought us into the kingdom of the Son he loves, in whom we have redemption, the forgiveness of sins" (Colossians 1:13-14). The passage is describing the best human migration possible, from one kingdom to another, from slavery into the refuge of God. Now, how many kingdoms are named here? Only two: the Kingdom of God and the kingdom of darkness. From God's perspective there are only two kingdoms or "countries" in this universe. Did you see any other options mentioned here? There is God's Kingdom or Satan's. That's it. Those are your choices.*
>
> —John Eldredge, *Experience Jesus. Really.*[28] (scripture reference added)

---

28. Taken from *Experience Jesus. Really.* by John Eldredge Copyright © 2025 by John Eldredge. Used by permission of HarperCollins Christian Publishing. www.harpercollinschristian.com.

If we have been snatched from the jaws of death and brought into God's Kingdom by faith in Jesus, then let's choose to root out anything in our lives that keeps us from being loyal citizens of that Kingdom.

Where are you in the sanctification process? If, in fact, you have decided to follow Jesus. Do you need to develop more self-control, fight against your spiritual complacency, fix your eyes on Jesus, get a spiritual workout plan in place, or clear out some distractions? The survival instincts we've gone through in the last two chapters are just a few of the areas in life where we need to rely on God to help us. Again, ask God to show you these and any other areas where He wants you to grow. Then, take that step of faith to follow Him, trusting where He leads.

Think outside the box. Don't just go along with life like everyone else.

Fight for your faith!

QUESTIONS

- What or who is distracting me from a deeper relationship to God?

- What am I going to do about it?

- Do I care more about things of the world than I do about God?

PRAYER

Father, help me clear out any distractions that are keeping me away from You. Holy Spirit, convict me about the areas You want to change, and give me the power to do it so I can bear good fruit for the furtherance of Your Kingdom and Your will on the earth, just like it is in heaven. In Jesus's mighty name. Amen!

Chapter 7

PERSPECTIVE

That is why we never give up. Though our bodies are dying, our spirits are being renewed every day. For our present troubles are small and won't last very long. Yet they produce for us a glory that vastly outweighs them and will last forever! So we don't look at the troubles we can see now; rather, we fix our gaze on things that cannot be seen. For the things we see now will soon be gone, but the things we cannot see will last forever.

—2 Corinthians 4:16-18

It was 5:45 a.m., and our day shift patrol unit was in roll call—drinking coffee, going over things, and getting ready for our upcoming twelve-hour shift—when the call came out: a wreck with injuries at one of the major intersections in our small city. We went from relaxing and trying to wake up to running out the door and turning our lights and sirens on. The scene wasn't far from our police department, and I was one of the first to arrive.

It wasn't good.

It was still dark outside, but we could see the car was a mangled mess in the middle of the intersection. Initially, after getting to a scene, we must quickly assess the situation so we can do all we can to preserve life. A quick scan of the wreck seemed to reveal that a large 18-wheeler had collided with a small car. The car was smoking, and fluids were still leaking from it. We immediately rushed to the car and found we couldn't open the door because of the damage, so we broke the glass to gain access. We checked the vitals of the lady inside, who didn't appear to have had her seatbelt on, and determined she had already passed away, killed instantly by the collision. The truck driver had immediately pulled over to the side of the road and was physically OK but shaken up by the crash. It looked like the car attempted to make a left turn in front of the truck but unfortunately didn't make it. There were visible skid marks on the asphalt that corroborated the truck driver's statement of how he had tried to stop but was unable to because of the size of his truck.

At that point, we continued with the investigation of the collision by collecting the information needed and assisting other first responders on scene. I did my part and helped in any way I could before returning to patrol. It's so surreal to work on a tragedy like that and then just get on with your day. It affects you, but life goes on. That's one thing we've never been able to talk about much within the first responder's community—the accumulation of all the tragedies we must see and have to be a part of. It takes a toll, and if you don't have healthy ways of dealing with it, that's when you might turn to substances, relationships, and other destructive behaviors.

Afterward, my lieutenant approached me and asked if I saw the dash camera footage of the wreck from inside my patrol car. I told him I hadn't had a chance to look at it yet. He suggested I check it out and let him know what I think.

Once I got some time, I logged in to the camera system and watched the video.

It's one of those times when you know it's from God and not a coincidence.

Typically, once I turn my emergency lights on, the dash camera automatically turned on—and it was no different this time. I and the other officers got to the scene, lights flashing and radios blaring, trying to get the scene under control. Everything was very chaotic until a song came on the car radio. Normally with a scene like this, our police radios are constantly going off because of everything that's happening, but this time it was different. My car radio was tuned to the local Christian radio station, and I forgot to turn it down like I normally would. In the dash camera video, you can hear the car radio along with the police radio traffic. The song "In Better Hands" by Natalie Grant came on. Once the song started, the police radio traffic stopped. All you could hear was the sound of Natalie Grant singing about how her soul is flying even though she's on the ground and she's in "better hands now."[29]

I get chills every time I think about it. I was sitting there, watching my video in disbelief. The police radio traffic was silent up until the song ended, and then it started going again. It was a powerful moment to realize the lady that lost her life was, without a doubt, with Jesus in that moment.

After getting the proper permissions, the video was shared with the family of the woman who passed away. I wasn't able to be a part of that, but I hope God was able to bring some comfort to them amid this tragedy and through events I was a part of but had no control over. It's a humbling experience to be used by God in that way.

First responders see and experience so much trauma. We can begin to become jaded and emotionally numb by

29. C. Gravitt, J. Daddario, and T. Hardwell, "In Better Hands," on *Relentless*, Curb Records, 2007.

all we encounter. We can't wrap our heads around how there could be a loving God with so much evil in the world. It's a question everyone struggles with, and I hope you've gained a better understanding of sin and evil from the things we've discussed. Even though we can't understand it all on this side of heaven, God can redeem and bring something good out of the most horrific tragedies.

> *And we know that God causes everything to work together for the good of those who love God and are called according to his purpose for them.*
> —Romans 8:28

God's Word is truth. We must cling to it no matter how we feel.

ETERNAL PERSPECTIVE

Corrie Ten Boom had a great analogy that she would regularly use when trying to make sense out of suffering. She would compare our lives to a tapestry God is weaving. Our one life touches so many other lives throughout our time here. God effortlessly and perfectly weaves it all together for our good and His glory.

> *Such knowledge is too wonderful for me, too great for me to understand!*
> —Psalm 139:6

We only see a small portion and have a limited understanding of the grand masterpiece God is creating. Right now, from our perspective, it's like looking at a small, specific section of the tapestry—from the back. If you've ever seen something like that from the back side, it looks like a jumbled mess, but if you view it from the front, seeing the entire tapestry, you understand and appreciate everything that went into creating it. One day, all will be revealed, and we will know exactly why things had to happen the way they did. Until then, we are called to trust Him with our lives. For me, understanding this perspective was beneficial for my personal and professional life alike.

Another helpful way to view life from an eternal perspective is recognizing that the things we believe we own or control are really an illusion. We don't truly possess anything—everything we have is a gift from God. He is sovereign, in control of all things, and everything ultimately belongs to Him.

> *For all the world is mine and everything in it.*
> —Psalms 50:12b

The sovereignty of God is a deep subject and something, I believe, we'll never completely understand this side of heaven; however, my pastor has used an excellent analogy to help wrap our heads around it. Imagine God's sovereignty as banks of a river. These are His plans that have been set in place and will not be moved. We are in the river and flowing to the ultimate destination that God has determined. While in the river, we have our free will to choose how we will live our lives here and now. The choices we make will affect ourselves and others in eternity, but God has charted a course for human history, and there's nothing we can do to stop it.

How are you going to use the time you've been given? Ultimately, we are going to leave this world in the same way we came into it. We arrived with nothing, and we're going to leave with nothing. Our only hope after death is going to be in Jesus.

I think all first responders can relate, but for me, as a police officer, it was always easier to fulfill my oath to protect than it was to serve. Protection is noble, necessary, and exciting. Service requires humility and is usually something no one wants to do. Seeing life from an eternal perspective has helped spur me on to fulfill my oath to protect *and* serve, since I know God can use me to bring good out of all the evil. I believe it could be helpful for all of us to change our perspective and see our profession from a more service-oriented view. All first responders know they *have* to serve the public, but how many of us truly *want* to serve the public?

As a follower of Jesus, service is part of the package, so it really fits into what we should be doing as first responders. In John 13:1-17, Jesus demonstrates by washing His disciples' feet how we are supposed to serve others. It's an illustration of humble leadership—being willing to do the job no one else wants to do purely because we love God and want to love others.

Being servant leaders also leads to questions about our relationship with God in the way of service and obedience. We know we *have* to obey God, but how many of us *want* to obey God? To do what God wants us to do because we love Him and not out of obligation? We talk about loving God, but at the same time we won't do what He says. Is that real love?

> *If you love me, obey my commandments.*
> —John 14:15

We also know in our heads that God's Word says He loves us, but how many of us truly believe in our hearts that God loves us? That He takes great delight in us and rejoices over us with singing (see Zephaniah 3:17)?

I hope God can use these insights to give you a new perspective. Pray, right now, that God would help you know how deeply He loves you. From that heart knowledge of being loved by God, the Holy Spirit can then help us see life from an eternal perspective and empower us to love and serve God and others.

Back when I was on patrol as a field training officer (FTO), when a new or "rookie" officer started I was responsible for helping get that person trained and ready to work on patrol. There were two questions I would always ask them before we went over anything else:

1. Are you mentally prepared to take a life if you must?
2. Are you mentally prepared to die?

Those are both heavy questions, but they are ultimately the hardest things we would have to do in our profession as law enforcement officers. Concerning preparation and training, the Navy Seals understand this idea. They teach that you will not elevate yourself to what is happening around you. You will inevitably do what you have trained and prepared to do. Whatever that preparation, or lack thereof, would be. There is no way you can fully prepare, but if you can train mentally, spiritually, and physically for the hardest parts of your job, I believe you can have a great career as a first responder.

We can ask ourselves a similar question spiritually: *Am I spiritually prepared to die?*

We are not here on this earth for very long. The Bible is clear about that.

> *O Lord, what are human beings that you should notice them, mere mortals that you should think about them? For they are like a breath of air; their days are like a passing shadow.*
>
> —Psalm 144:3-4

> *For we were born but yesterday and know nothing. Our days on earth are as fleeting as a shadow.*
>
> —Job 8:9

A voice said, "Shout!", I asked, "What should I shout?" "Shout that people are like the grass. Their beauty fades as quickly as the flowers in a field. The grass withers and the flowers fade beneath the breath of the Lord. *And so it is with people. The grass withers and the flowers fade, but the word of our God stands forever.*
—Isaiah 40:6-8

Teach us to realize the brevity of life, so that we may grow in wisdom.
—Psalm 90:12

Look here, you who say, "Today or tomorrow we are going to a certain town and will stay there a year. We will do business there and make a profit." How do you know what your life will be like tomorrow? Your life is like the morning fog—it's here a little while, then it's gone. What you ought to say is, "If the Lord wants us to, we will live and do this or that." Otherwise you are boasting about your own pretentious plans, and all such boasting is evil.
—James 4:13-16

In the scope of eternity, we are here for just a little while, like the morning fog. It's meant to be a sobering thought, waking us up to the reality of what's important. As first responders, we are confronted with this regularly. Every time you work a shift, you never know what's going to happen. When you approach a vehicle on a traffic stop. When you respond to that domestic situation. When you get to that structure fire. When you're trying to give an uncooperative person medical assistance in a dangerous area. When you're boxing with shadows in the trenches of your mind. We never know when your last moment will be. But we have to continue on nonetheless. It's the job we signed up for, right?

So, since our lives are brief in light of eternity, how much more should we look to our Heavenly Father for provision and guidance now? To be about His Kingdom business and furthering His will? Our lives are fragile, but we can place our faith in a God whose "power is absolute!" and whose "understanding is beyond comprehension!" (Psalm 147:5).

My favorite movie is Gladiator. The story and action are excellent, and although the film isn't told from a Christian perspective, it still highlights values such as loyalty, integrity, and honor. Early in the movie, Maximus, the main character, motivates his soldiers by reminding them that the choices they make and the actions they take in this life will echo into eternity. No matter how small or insignificant your life may feel, what you do truly matters. I love how that idea keeps me grounded and mindful of how I'm living and the lasting impact my choices can have.

There is also a powerful scene where Maximus and his new friend, Juba, talk together on a rooftop one evening. They share their longing to be reunited with their families and reflect on what awaits us after death. Maximus says that his wife and son are already waiting for him in the afterlife. Juba gently encourages him, assuring him that he will see them again one day—just not yet. Maximus still has things he must accomplish in this life before that reunion comes.[30]

Yes, one day we will all die—*but not yet.*

If you have turned from sin and are following Jesus, then heaven is your home. One day we will see Him face to face, and all will be made right. *But not yet.* One day we will close our eyes on earth and open them in heaven. *But not yet.* If you're still breathing, it's not too late, and we have work

30. R. Scott, *Gladiator*, film (Universal City, CA: DreamWorks Pictures, Universal Pictures; Los Angeles: Scott Free Productions, Red Wagon Entertainment, 2000).

to do! We should be about the Father's business of bringing His Kingdom to this desperate world right now, while we can. Press on through the night with Jesus by your side and as your light.

POWER AND AUTHORITY

I truly believe God uses and protects first responders in so many ways and for so many reasons, whether they know it or not. There have been countless times when I was *in the right place, at the right time*, where God protected me while I was on shift. I bet you have similar times like this as well, where something happened that you just can't explain, and you knew God was watching over you. I have no doubt there have also been many instances of protection from my Heavenly Father that I am completely unaware of. As one psalm says,

> *The Lord himself watches over you! The Lord stands beside you as your protective shade.*
> —Psalm 121:5

Many law enforcement officers are somewhat familiar with these verses:

> *Everyone must submit to governing authorities. For all authority comes from God, and those in positions of authority have been placed there by God. So anyone who rebels against authority is rebelling against what God has instituted, and they will be punished. For the authorities do not strike fear in people who are doing right, but in those who are doing wrong. Would you like to live without fear of the authorities? Do what is right, and they will honor you. The authorities are God's servants, sent for your good. But if you*

are doing wrong, of course you should be afraid, for they have the power to punish you. They are God's servants, sent for the very purpose of punishing those who do what is wrong. So you must submit to them, not only to avoid punishment, but also to keep a clear conscience.
—Romans 13:1-5

According to the Bible, the governing authorities are placed there by God. There are some parts of these verses directed specifically to professions like law enforcement and military service; however, I feel like it also extends to all first responders because we're all placed there by some governing authority for the purpose of civil service. God is with us for that reason. However, on the flip side of that, since it is meant to be a noble and God-honoring profession, Satan would love to destroy what God has put in place. I think that's why first responders can have such a tough time. When we try to fight a supernatural battle under our own natural power, it won't work. If we don't operate from faith in Jesus, we're at risk of being a casualty in this spiritual war. What a great responsibility it is to be a part of what God has put in place. We should not take our roles as first responders lightly.

"When someone has been given much, much will be required in return; and when someone has been entrusted with much, even more will be required."
—Luke 12:48b

Or, if you prefer, the idea from *Spider-Man* that greater abilities place a greater responsibility on the one who has them.[31]

We all have a calling from God on our lives—His purposes that He desires to accomplish through us. It's up

31. S. Lee, *Amazing Fantasy* no. 15 (New York: Marvel Comics, 1962).

to us to decide whether or not we are going to seek after the Father, allowing Him to reveal to us what those purposes are and then deciding to walk obediently in the direction God has shown us. God called you into the first responder profession for a reason, and it is an honorable role in service to the public.

As first responders, are we going to use our authority or position of trust from a godly perspective, or are we going to use it for selfish reasons? I've seen both throughout my time in law enforcement. From just selfishly not wanting to serve the public in some small way to breaking the law and suffering the consequences. Even if we don't go to the extreme of breaking the law, our lives could still suffer if we're not operating from the firm foundation of faith in Jesus.

If we follow Jesus as first responders, we are going to stand out—especially if you've been one of the "problem children" in the agency. We all know those kinds of people. I was one to a certain degree. Before I started following Jesus, I just went along with the crowd. I talked how they talked, did what they did. Once God changed me, I was a completely different person, and people noticed. I started hearing word around the department that they thought I had turned into a "holier than thou" hypocrite. They were wondering how I could think I was godly when I had been acting just like them. Because I was in a position of leadership there, God led me to write and post a letter at the department, explaining the change. Thankfully, God used that to help people understand my heart and where I was coming from. People are going to respond differently to you when they know you are trying to surrender your entire life to Jesus and follow Him with your whole heart. The world is not going to understand.

That's OK.

It shouldn't matter what they think. We should still love and care for others. The only thing that matters is what God thinks of you. If you turned away from sin to follow

Him, then He is for you and not against you. And, "If God is for us, who can ever be against us?" (Romans 8:31b).

This is how A. W. Tozer says it:

> *The moment we make up our minds that we are going on with this determination to exalt God over all, we step out of the world's parade. We shall find ourselves out of adjustment to the ways of the world, and increasingly so, as we make progress in the holy way. We shall acquire a new viewpoint; a new and different psychology will be formed within us; a new power will begin to surprise us by its upsurgings and its outgoings.*
>
> *Our break with the world will be the direct outcome of our changed relationship to God. For the world of fallen men does not honor God. Millions call themselves by His name, it is true, and pay some token respect to Him, but a simple test will show how little He is really honored among them. Let the average man be put to the proof on the question of who is above, and his true position will be exposed. Let him be forced into making a choice between God and money, between God and men, between God and personal ambition, God and self, God and human love, and God will take second place every time. Those other things will be exalted above. However the man may protest, the proof is in the choices he makes day after day throughout his life.*
>
> —A. W. Tozer, *The Pursuit of God* [32]

There are two really interesting stories in the Gospels about two very different types of Roman soldiers that help

32. A. W. Tozer, *The Pursuit of God* (1948; repr., Abbotsford, WI: Aneko Press, 2015). Used with permission.

with this idea of having a unique perspective as a follower of Jesus. There were the Roman soldiers who put themselves in authority over Jesus to hurt and mock Him, and there was the Roman soldier who placed himself under Jesus's authority and believed in Him.

Back when Jesus was on Earth, Rome was in charge and had power over the Jewish people. The Jews did not care for Roman authority at all, hoping the Messiah would come to deliver them from Roman oppression. Jesus did, in fact, come to deliver them and the whole world, but not in the way they were expecting.

There are a few stories of Roman soldiers in the Gospels, and I can't help but put myself in their shoes because they were Gentiles (non-Jews) and the enforcers of law during that time. How would I have responded to Jesus if I were a Roman soldier during that time? Would I have been one of the soldiers who mocked, beat, scourged, or executed Him? It's true, they had been given orders to do that; however, they relished in their supposed authority over Jesus by making a crown of thorns and placing a purple robe on Him. Then kneeled in mock worship to the "King of the Jews," as they referred to Him. Later, they stripped Jesus naked and "cast lots"—kind of like flipping a coin—for His clothing, which could have been valuable (see Mark 15).

Or, would I have been more like the Roman centurion, a commander of a regiment of one hundred soldiers, who sent for Jesus, requesting that He heal a servant he cared for (Luke 7:1-10)? The centurion sent his Jewish friends to ask Jesus not to come to his home because he wasn't worthy of such an honor. The centurion even felt like he was unworthy to come and meet with Jesus! The centurion's friends went on to explain that the centurion knew how authority worked because if he told someone to go and do something, they would go and do it. The centurion knew if Jesus would just say the word, his servant would be healed.

> *When Jesus heard this, he was amazed. Turning to the crowd that was following him, he said, "I tell you, I haven't seen faith like this in all Israel!" And when the officer's friends returned to his house, they found the slave completely healed.*
>
> —Luke 7:9-10

This Roman centurion had faith. He knew he had some authority on this Earth, but he humbled himself under the all-powerful authority of Jesus. We should find ourselves in this duality as well. Because of our sins, Jesus was beaten and executed; but, because of what Jesus did for us, we can have miraculous faith.

Since we've been talking about having a different perspective as followers of Jesus, consider the perspective the Roman soldiers had. The ones beating and executing Jesus didn't seem to care one bit about anything else other than doing their job and going along with the flow of what everyone else was doing. *Hey, it's my job. This is what I get paid for, and, besides, my boss told me to do it. What do you expect me to do?* Does that sound familiar? What about the Roman centurion? He risked his reputation, job, and family for his faith in Jesus.

Are we willing to do that?

QUESTIONS

- What is my perspective on this life?

- As a first responder, have I been inexplicably protected or spared from something? Should I be grateful to God for that?

- Am I more concerned about what other people think of me or what God thinks of me?

- Which Roman soldier story and their view of Jesus do I identify with most?

PRAYER

Father, change my perspective on this life. Show me how brief my time is here, and let that bring me closer to You. I am a fragile clay jar, and You are the Rock of Ages. Give me an honest view of myself so that I can begin to see You in all Your glory. Free me completely of any concern over what others think of me. Let my desire be to love You and love others like You do. I want Your Kingdom to come and Your will to be done right now. Continue to strengthen my faith as I seek to know You more. In Jesus's name. Amen.

Chapter 8

COURAGE

But when I am afraid,
I will put my trust in you.
I praise God for what he has promised.
I trust in God, so why should I be afraid?
What can mere mortals do to me?

—Psalm 56:3-4

Stay close to me as I'm fed to the flames
When I get to the other side I know dawn awaits
Together, whatever, through this suffering
I know I will rise
There were four in the fire

—Meet Your Maker, "In The Fire"[33]

Our department's Special Response or Special Weapons and Tactical (SWAT) team got called out on a suicidal

33. D. Myhill and M. McKay, "In the Fire," on *Hallowed*, Meet Your Maker, 2025, used with permission.

subject in an apartment one evening. This specific call stands out because it was the first time I was the first in line on the entry team. Officers on the patrol shift had tried to talk with him, but he locked himself inside and said he wasn't coming out. We established contact with the subject and made the area as safe as possible for the public while we negotiated with the guy inside. We had no reason to believe anyone else was inside the apartment, so our crisis negotiator attempted to talk him through what was going on so we could try to help him.

After a while, we stopped receiving any communication from him, so we deployed a robot to see what we could determine about the situation. It was a small mobile robot that could be thrown through a window. We broke the window and threw the robot in to surveil the area. There was still no response from the guy inside. Unfortunately, the robot was thrown where they could not maneuver it well enough to get a good view of the subject or the layout of the apartment. After a period of trying to get the robot to work, and still hearing no response from the guy, the decision was made to make entry into the apartment.

Most law enforcement will be familiar with how this works, but we had an operator designated for breaching the door (which is just a way of saying he was going to swing a heavy tool against the door to force it open). The breacher was opposite me, and we had to communicate with each other beforehand so we could time the entry appropriately. Once he was able to get the door open, the entry team had to clear and secure the apartment before any medical personnel could come in.

During the time before entry, my senses were on fire. I rehearsed in my head everything that I needed to be focused on to make sure I wouldn't be a weak link within the team—previous trainings that dealt with weapon retention, staying out of the fatal funnel, steady breathing, clearing corners, filling the gap, and so on.

Time seemed to slow down just before the breacher slammed the door open, and I led our team into the apartment. The first thing we encountered was blood on the linoleum floor where he had been cutting himself, and the guy was on the couch in the living area unconscious. My boots started slipping in the blood, but I didn't stop. I had to make sure the team was safely covered in case there was anyone else inside the apartment. Two of my teammates covered down on the guy to make sure he wasn't a threat, and the rest of us did the job of clearing the apartment. The remainder of my time there was a bit of a blur because I was still amped up on adrenaline, but we finished the entry and were able to get medical personnel inside the apartment to look after the guy. If my memory serves me correctly, the guy was still alive, and they were able to get him to the hospital to get him some help. It was a great example of first responders working together to help someone in a dark moment.

It did take courage to do what we did that day; however, I think there is a greater form of courage. I have two favorite stories from the Bible that have spoken to me over the years. One is from the Old Testament book of Daniel, in chapter 3—the story of Shadrach, Meshach, and Abednego and the fiery furnace. The other is in Matthew where Peter denies knowing Jesus (we will discuss this one in the next chapter). I'd like to share some truths that God has given to me through His Word, specifically from these stories. Remember, God's Word is "alive and powerful" (Hebrews 4:12), and He wants to reveal His truths to you.

THE FIERY FURNACE

The story of the fiery furnace in Daniel 3 is a good one if you haven't read it before. Essentially, the pagan King

Nebuchadnezzar had ordered everyone to bow down to the huge golden statue of himself he had made or else be thrown into a fiery furnace. Shadrach, Meshach, and Abednego—three warriors of God—refused to do so, and the king became angry but gave them a second chance to bow down to his idol.

> *Shadrach, Meshach, and Abednego replied, "O Nebuchadnezzar, we do not need to defend ourselves before you. If we are thrown into the blazing furnace, the God whom we serve is able to save us. He will rescue us from your power, Your Majesty. But even if he doesn't, we want to make it clear to you, Your Majesty, that we will never serve your gods or worship the gold statue you have set up."*
>
> —Daniel 3:16-18

> *Thrown to the flames, you will only hear my song of praise*
> *If to live is Christ then to die is gain*
> *The grave will be my slave*
> *So throw me to the flames*
>
> —Meet Your Maker, "In the Fire"[34]

The first thing that always stood out to me is the courage of these men to stand up to a king and his kingdom and to be willing to die for the truth. This was not an easy thing to do. It's not like they woke up that morning and decided they would make a stand for God. They had been building that spiritual foundation for years while living in exile away from their homes. Because of their consistent walk with the Lord, they feared and honored God more than man.

34. D. Myhill and M. McKay, "In the Fire," on *Hallowed*, Meet Your Maker, 2025, used with permission.

> *The fear of man lays a snare, but whoever trusts in the Lord is safe.*
>
> —Proverbs 29:25 ESV

> *"Don't be afraid of those who want to kill your body; they cannot touch your soul. Fear only God, who can destroy both soul and body in hell."*
>
> —Matthew 10:28

This speaks directly to my tendency to want to please everyone and make everyone like me. If I care more about that than pleasing God, I will be the one to compromise my faith and bow before the golden statue. There are some times when you must stand up regardless of the consequences because you know it's what God would want you to do. It reminds me of something Captain America said in the comics. He's talking with Spider-Man and explains that it doesn't matter what anyone says if they're trying to convince you that something wrong is something right. If the whole world tells you that you must do something wrong, your job is to stay planted like a tree by the river of truth and tell the world *no, you've got to move.*[35]

It also brings to mind this Scripture:

> *Oh, the joys of those who do not follow the advice of the wicked, or stand around with sinners, or join in with mockers. But they delight in the law of the Lord, meditating on it day and night. They are like trees planted along the riverbank, bearing fruit each season. Their leaves never wither, and they prosper in all they do.*
>
> —Psalm 1:1-3

35. J. M. Straczynski, *Amazing Spider-Man* no. 537 (New York: Marvel Comics, 2007).

These faithful men had been meditating on and delighting in the law of the Lord, so they were prepared to take a stand, ready and willing to die for God. Don't miss this: they had faith that God would save them, but they were ready to die in obedience to God. That's powerful and should make us take a humble look within ourselves to see if our faith is strong and true, not dependent on ourselves but dependent on the Creator of everything.

If we had been put in their position, what would we have done? When someone is talking against God, are you tempted to just go with the flow? Or would you, with love and truth, stand strong in the faith? If your honest answer is, "No, I'm not willing to stand up for my faith in Jesus," then, please . . .

> *Examine yourselves to see if your faith is genuine. Test yourselves. Surely you know that Jesus Christ is among you; if not, you have failed the test of genuine faith.*
>
> —2 Corinthians 13:5

We have already discussed what true faith in Jesus looks like. Examine your life honestly in the light of the truth, and decide how you want to live your life.

After their stand against the king, the king was furious! He ordered some of his strongest men to tie up Shadrach, Meshach, and Abednego and throw them into the furnace. Because the king had been so angry with them, he had the fire heated up seven times hotter than normal. It was so hot it killed the men that threw them in there!

Talking about this fiery furnace reminds me of an accident scene I responded to. It was reported the car was on fire, so I got there as fast as I could and saw where the car engine was ablaze. I quickly checked inside, discovering that everyone had thankfully made it out safely. Then I saw the brave firefighters topping the hill in their big, shiny truck, with lights flashing and sirens blaring, coming to rescue us all from the fire. I knew they had seen the smoke and were getting amped up. I couldn't get to the back of my trunk quick enough, where I grabbed my fire extinguisher and raced back to the inferno. I gave one more look back at the fire truck before dousing the flames. Of course, I had to rub it in once they got there.

"Don't worry, guys. I took care of the fire. Everyone's safe now."

They looked at me and just shook their heads, saying, "You know every police officer dreams of being a firefighter anyways, right?" The relationship between police officers and firefighters, in my experience, has been sort of like a sibling rivalry. We like to give each other a hard time but would do anything to help the other.

Well, my puny fire extinguisher wouldn't have worked on the fiery furnace, and I'm sure Nebuchadnezzar thought our boys had been instantly killed. However, he quickly realized something miraculous was happening. He freaked out when he saw them still alive and glimpsed a fourth man in the fire with them that "look[ed] like a god!" (Daniel 3:25b). The ESV translation of that same verse says the fourth man looked "like a son of the gods." Many scholars believe that Jesus was the one in the furnace with them, protecting them and saving them through this violent trial.

The king called for them to come out of the fire. They came out just fine, not even smelling like smoke. The king was amazed and changed by what he had experienced.

> *Then Nebuchadnezzar said, "Praise to the God of Shadrach, Meshach, and Abednego! He sent his angel to rescue his servants who trusted in him. They defied the king's command and were willing to die rather than serve or worship any*

> *god except their own God. Therefore, I make this decree: If any people, whatever their race or nation or language, speak a word against the God of Shadrach, Meshach, and Abednego, they will be torn limb from limb, and their houses will be turned into heaps of rubble. There is no other god who can rescue like this!"*
>
> —Daniel 3:28-29

Because of their faith, God miraculously delivered them. As a result, His greatness was proclaimed by a king to a nation of unbelievers.

How many opportunities from God are we missing because we're scared, we're not paying attention, or we just want to *go along to get along*? This is a humbling question for me, and it motivates me to depend more on the Holy Spirit in my everyday life. There is grace for our failures, as we'll see in the next chapter, but I want to be someone who will never waver in the face of adversity—ready to die for the sake of the gospel of Jesus.

QUESTIONS

- Am I willing to die for Jesus?

- Have I been trusting in myself to deliver me from life's problems?

- How much time have I wasted or how many opportunities have I missed to help others because I was scared or apathetic?

PRAYER

Lord, forgive me for my lack of courage and for my fear of people or circumstances. The fear does not come from You but from the evil one. I know You want to empower me to follow You in every area of my life and to give me the strength and power I need to live out my faith. Help me to stand firm by the river of truth, trusting that You will deliver me through the fiery furnace of life. Thank You for Your faithful and loving presence. I ask this in Jesus's name and by the power of the Holy Spirit. Amen.

Chapter 9

GRACE IN FAILURE

So God can point to us in all future ages as examples of the incredible wealth of His grace and kindness toward us, as shown in all he has done for us who are united with Christ Jesus.

—Ephesians 2:7

We all want to be like the guys in the fiery furnace—stepping up with courage and facing whatever obstacles may come our way.

No matter what.

The truth is, however, a lot of the time, despite our great intentions, we fail to do the things we really want to.

> *I don't really understand myself, for I want to do what is right, but I don't do it. Instead, I do what I hate. . . . And I know that nothing*

> *good lives in me, that is, in my sinful nature. I want to do what is right, but I can't. I want to do what is good, but I don't. I don't want to do what is wrong, but I do it anyway.*
>
> —Romans 7:15, 18-19

This is why I love Peter. He is relatable in so many ways. Peter's denial of Jesus is recorded in all four Gospels—Matthew, Mark, Luke, and John—but only John includes the intimate conversation where Jesus gently restores and heals Peter after his failure.

Peter was one of Jesus's closest disciples.

> *Peter first confessed Jesus as "the Christ, the Son of the living God," a truth which Jesus said was divinely revealed to Peter (Matthew 16:16-17). He was one of three (the others were James and John) present when Jesus raised the daughter of Jairus (Mark 5:37), when Jesus was transfigured on the mountain (Matthew 17:1), and Peter and John were given the special task of preparing the final Passover meal (Luke 22:8).*[36]

However, Peter was surely imperfect. He previously boasted,

> *"Even if everyone else deserts you, I will never desert you."*
>
> —Matthew 26:33b

This is after Jesus told them they would all desert Him because the Scriptures foretold it. Jesus told him,

> *"I tell you the truth, Peter—this very night, before the rooster crows, you will deny three*

36. "Who Was Peter in the Bible?" *GotQuestions.org*, accessed November 17, 2025, https://www.gotquestions.org/life-Peter.html. Used with permission.

> *times that you even know me." "No!" Peter insisted. "Even if I have to die with you, I will never deny you!" And all the other disciples vowed the same.*
>
> —Matthew 26:34-35

Peter truly believed Jesus was the Son of God but had the audacity to question the validity of what Jesus told him. Not long after this declaration and before the rooster crowed, Peter denied knowing Jesus three times. To me, the most striking account of this is in the Gospel of Luke. During Peter's third denial, the Scriptures say this:

> *And immediately, while he was still speaking, the rooster crowed. At that moment the Lord turned and looked at Peter. Suddenly, the Lord's words flashed through Peter's mind: "Before the rooster crows tomorrow morning, you will deny three times that you even know me." And Peter left the courtyard, weeping bitterly.*
>
> —Luke 22:60b-62

Can you imagine the feelings of guilt that came crashing down on Peter after locking eyes with Jesus? Unlike the Israelites in the fiery furnace story, Peter was afraid of people and what they would do to him. But that's why I like Peter so much—because I can relate to him. How many times have I said and done the exact opposite of what I know I should do or what I know to be true? How many times have I felt the crushing feelings of guilt, shame, and condemnation? How many times have I made a promise to myself and broken it?

Have you felt this way? Have you felt like you were too far gone to be saved? That the world would be better off without you?

I have. And I know I'm not alone.

Thankfully the story doesn't end there. After Jesus's death, Peter goes right back to what he was doing before he met Jesus—working as a fisherman.

> *Simon Peter said, "I'm going fishing." "We'll come, too," they all said. So they went out in the boat, but they caught nothing all night.*
>
> —John 21:3-4

Even though Peter had already seen the resurrected Jesus, it's almost like Peter was lost and just went back to what he knew he could do. The Jewish people had always been waiting for their Messiah to come save them and set up His eternal Kingdom, but, like I mentioned, Jesus was not what they were expecting. Even though Isaiah talked about how the Messiah must suffer and die (see Isaiah 52:13-15 and Isaiah 53), they still believed His Kingdom would be a mighty earthly Kingdom and not the way Jesus talked about it. Yes, Peter had declared that Jesus was the Christ, the Son of the living God, and he truly believed that. However, I think he underestimated God.

We do that too much.

This is the same God who created the universe with just a word (Genesis 1). The same God who split the Red Sea (Exodus 14), kept three young Hebrew men from burning to death in a fiery furnace (Daniel 3), and helped a young shepherd defeat a giant (1 Samuel 17). God doesn't do things our way or how we think they should be done. Peter and the rest of the disciples had placed God in a box and failed to see what was right in front of them.

Peter didn't know what to do with himself. He was still feeling guilty for denying Jesus, so he went back to what he knew he could do; but when he tried, they didn't catch any fish all night.

He was a failure at that too.

I bet that was a long night for all of them. They spent three years with Jesus and had left everything behind to follow Him. Now He was dead, and they didn't know what to do. Were they worried because their leader had died, and they could be next? I wonder if it was just a silent night—letting their hands do the work they were used to doing before they met Jesus. Maybe getting agitated and frustrated with each other because they weren't catching anything. Thinking about how things had gotten this bad and if they could've done anything to stop it. Missing and grieving over their teacher and friend. Yeah, that would've been a long night.

Then the day breaks.

> *At dawn Jesus was standing on the beach, but the disciples couldn't see who he was. He called out, "Fellows, have you caught any fish?" "No," they replied. Then he said, "Throw out your net on the right-hand side of the boat, and you'll get some!" So they did, and they couldn't haul in the net because there were so many fish in it.*
>
> —John 21:4-6

I love how Jesus sought out his friends, like a good shepherd would with any lost sheep. And this conversation was just like Jesus. He didn't walk up and say, "Hey, guys. It's me, Jesus! I rose from the dead, and I'm OK!" Instead, Jesus walked up and performed the same miracle He did when He first met Peter (see Luke 5:1-11). So when Jesus asked them if they had caught anything, all they said was, "No"—probably not paying Him any attention, tired and frustrated from a long night of fruitless labor. He then miraculously filled their nets with fish again to try and help them remember. He knew how prone they were (and we are) to go back to what they/we are familiar with and forget what God has done in our lives.

It worked. John recognized Jesus first. (Quick side note: John described himself in the book he wrote as "the disciple Jesus loved." John had become settled in his identity and knew who he was in Christ.)

> *Then the disciple Jesus loved said to Peter, "It's the Lord!" When Simon Peter heard that it was the Lord, he put on his tunic (for he had stripped for work), jumped into the water, and headed to shore. The others stayed with the boat and pulled the loaded net to the shore, for they were only about a hundred yards from shore. When they got there, they found breakfast waiting for them—fish cooking over a charcoal fire, and some bread. "Bring some of the fish you've just caught," Jesus said. So Simon Peter went aboard and dragged the net to the shore. There were 153 large fish, and yet the net hadn't torn. "Now come and have some breakfast!" Jesus said. None of the disciples dared to ask him, "Who are you?" They knew it was the Lord. Then Jesus served them the bread and the fish. This was the third time Jesus had appeared to his disciples since he had been raised from the dead.*
>
> —John 21:7-14

When Peter realized who it was, he couldn't contain his excitement! He threw his coat on and jumped in the water to get to Jesus. He couldn't wait to see Him. Another interesting point to me is it appears Jesus had already been there a while, preparing breakfast for them. Watching them struggle in the boat and waiting for the right time to reveal Himself. He knew they would be hungry and tired, and He wanted to be there for them.

To *serve* them breakfast.

Even as our risen Lord and Savior, He is still serving, and He wants us to follow His lead.

By the way, where did Jesus get the fish He was cooking? The text said Jesus had some fish cooked and bread ready for them. I don't know where it came from, but it's a pretty cool detail in the story.

I do wonder what they talked about over breakfast. Or if they even talked at all. The famous preacher Charles Spurgeon commented on it this way:

> *They ate the bread and fish that morning, I doubt not, in silent self-humiliation. Peter looked with tears in his eyes at that fire of coals, remembering how he stood and warmed himself when he denied his Master. Thomas stood there, wondering that he should have dared to ask such proofs of a fact most clear. All of them felt that they could shrink into nothing in his divine presence, since they had behaved so ill.*
> —Charles Spurgeon, *Breakfast with Jesus* [37]

Then, after they had finished eating, Jesus turned His attention to Peter in front of all the other disciples.

> *After breakfast Jesus asked Simon Peter, "Simon son of John, do you love me more than these?" "Yes, Lord," Peter replied, "you know I love you." "Then feed my lambs," Jesus told him. Jesus repeated the question: "Simon son of John, do you love me?" "Yes, Lord," Peter said, "you know I love you." "Then take care of my sheep," Jesus said. A third time he asked him, "Simon son of John, do you love me?" Peter was hurt that*

37. C. H. Spurgeon, "Breakfast with Jesus," *Metropolitan Tabernacle Pulpit*, vol. 35, February 24, 1889, https://www.spurgeon.org/resource-library/sermons/breakfast-with-jesus/#flipbook/. Used with permission.

> *Jesus asked the question a third time. He said, "Lord, you know everything. You know that I love you." Jesus said, "Then feed my sheep."*
> —John 21:15-17

I think Peter was hurt because he knew why Jesus asked him a third time, but Jesus was lovingly restoring Peter to relationship with Himself in front of the others to give him confidence going forward. Jesus graciously gave Peter the second chance to profess his love for Him in front of others in order to help Peter overcome the shame of denying Him. I love this. We've all made a mess of things in our lives. No one is perfect, but God is. He is always faithful, even when we aren't, and He is waiting for us to turn to Him in faith and seek His Kingdom above everything else in this life.

Because of this restoration and after receiving the Holy Spirit, Peter went on to be a strong pillar of the church and was later martyred for his faith. Even through his failure, he didn't give up. He continued following Jesus, even to his death. When Peter woke up in heaven, I bet he ran to Jesus just like he did before, and I am certain he heard the words of his Master say,

> *"Well done, my good and faithful servant."*
> —Matthew 25:21

THE HELP WE NEED

We've discussed two amazing stories from the Bible in these last two chapters. In the first story, Shadrach, Meshach, and Abednego had courage and were successful in standing strong in their faith, no matter what. In the story of Peter, we saw that Peter failed to hang on to faith when it mattered the most. The powerful truth is, Jesus was in the middle of both of these stories. He was literally in the middle of the fire, strengthening their faith and using it to bring a pagan nation into knowledge of the living God. He came back for Peter—to seek and save His lost sheep as the Good Shepherd—when Peter needed Him most of all. Jesus then used Peter in a mighty way to share His Good News with the world. Jesus was in the middle of their stories, and He is in the middle of yours too. No matter how bad it is, God is right there with you, waiting for you to turn to Him in faith.

There are different ways that courage shows up in a person's life. Does it take courage to walk into harm's way, regardless of the consequences? Absolutely! But it also takes courage to talk about how the situations we deal with affect us and how we could be coping with it in the wrong ways—to face our failures head-on in the name of Jesus and by the power of the Spirit! Ironically enough, we, as first responders, tend to find it so much easier to risk our very lives than to admit our failings and seek help.

Asking for help can be hard, but there was (at least) one time I'm really glad I did.

I've always had a sense of how much I depended on dispatchers and correctional officers. Their help on a call or afterwards when dealing with a subject that has been arrested is invaluable. We don't give them enough credit, and their job can be a thankless one.

I had just arrested a guy—for what, I can't remember, but he did not appreciate the fact that I had deprived him of his freedom. He decided the best idea was to kick the cage in my patrol vehicle and scream obscenities and threats at me. I contacted the dispatcher over my radio and requested they contact the jail to give them a heads up about what I was dealing with. The dispatcher later told me she could barely make out what I was saying due to the guy yelling in the background.

On the way to the jail, while I was dealing with that, I gloved up, preparing to help the correctional officers deal with this knucklehead. As I was driving up to the sally port, which is where we drop off arrestees, I saw an incredibly encouraging sight. My dispatcher had been concerned and relayed the information very well because a large group of correctional officers were awaiting my arrival. The guy must've seen them too because he got quiet all of a sudden. I couldn't help but smile, appreciative of the support.

Well, I didn't even have time to get out of my vehicle. As soon as I stopped and unlocked the door, the officers grabbed the guy and physically carried him into the jail. They told me to just wait there while they got my handcuffs off the guy for me. When they walked back out with my handcuffs, I couldn't thank them enough for the help. It encouraged me, and I love telling the story when I can. Moral of the story: don't be afraid to ask for help!

Admitting we can't handle things on our own is one of the reasons it can be difficult to reach out for help. However, when we make that decision, we will usually find that others are ready and willing to help us bear the weight.

It takes courage to admit you need help. To have an honest conversation with Jesus and others we trust about where we are mentally and spiritually. To look inside yourself and admit you need to be saved from yourself before it's too late. To let the waves of God's amazing grace sweep you into the endless ocean of His love.

QUESTIONS

- What areas of my life do I need to step up with courage and deal with?

- What areas of my life do I need grace and forgiveness?

- Who can I talk to about that?

- Have I talked to God about it?

PRAYER

Jesus, forgive me for all the times I have failed You. I really want to follow You closely, but sometimes I mess up. In those times, I need Your love and grace more than ever. Help me own it, confess it, and turn from it so that I can continue to seek Your presence and will above all. I ask this in Jesus's name and by the power of the Holy Spirit. Amen.

Conclusion

PRESS THE FIGHT—DON'T BACK DOWN!

Oh, that we might know the Lord! Let us press on to know him. He will respond to us as surely as the arrival of dawn or the coming of rains in early spring.

—Hosea 6:3

Press on to know the Lord!

I love the confidence the writer of Hosea has in the Lord responding to those who pursue Him. If we will seek Him and His Kingdom above all else, the Lord will respond just as sure as the sun will rise in the morning or as the rains will come during spring.

I ran across an interesting fact about the word *decide*. According to one dictionary,[38] the word *decide* comes from

38. "Decide," *Online Etymology Dictionary*, accessed November 17, 2025, https://www.etymonline.com/word/decide

the Latin word *decider,* which literally means "to cut off." It's the idea of making a decision by cutting off other options. How applicable is that to the life of a believer? When we decide to follow Jesus, we cut off all other options—like Peter's response to Jesus after many other "disciples" turned away and left:

> *Then Jesus turned to the Twelve and asked, "Are you also going to leave?" Simon Peter replied, "Lord, to whom would we go? You have the words that give eternal life. We believe, and we know you are the Holy One of God."*
>
> —John 6:67-68

Let's *decide* to follow Jesus and cut off everything that is not eternal.

Progression toward perfection. We are called to be perfect like our Heavenly Father. We won't reach that goal in our lifetime; however, that is our goal, and, by the power of the Holy Spirit, we should pursue perfection because that is where we are headed as Christians.

> *"But you are to be perfect, even as your Father in heaven is perfect."*
>
> —Matthew 5:48

As a basketball coach, my wife says to her players, "You're either moving forward or backward, but you're never staying still." Either sin is pulling you down closer to death, or the Holy Spirit is making you alive and more like Jesus. There is no middle ground.

Our Father's goal for us is to sanctify and mold us to be more and more like Jesus every day. Our loving King Jesus has sent the Holy Spirit to all who are born again to help us in that journey on the narrow way. He literally takes up residence inside of us, and all we have to do is remain in Him in order to bear the fruit of the Spirit listed in Galatians 5.

Take up and gird yourself with the spiritual armor of God that Paul talks about in Ephesians 6.

> *A final word: Be strong in the Lord and in his mighty power. Put on all of God's armor so that you will be able to stand firm against all strategies of the devil.*
>
> —Ephesians 6:10-11

If we are to help bring God's Kingdom and will to this earth now, then this is the road we must take. I pray that the words on these pages have helped shine a light on what it really means to follow Jesus—that the Holy Spirit will move your heart to turn to Him and away from the sin that can so easily bring us down. The powerful name of Jesus is the only way we can find truth and life for us, our families, our colleagues, and the world.

Don't get distracted.

We are so easily pulled in different directions. We need reminders every day of who God is and what our purpose is. Every day, seek to hear from God through His Word, to talk to Him in prayer, and to love and forgive others just like God the Father loves and forgives you. We must invest in the things of heaven and not the things of this world. The things of this world will fade away, but the things of heaven are eternal and indestructible.

> *O my soul, do not set your affections upon rusting, moth-eaten, decaying treasures, but set your heart upon Him who remains forever faithful to you. Do not build your house upon the moving quicksands of a deceitful world, but base your hopes upon the Rock that will stand immovably secure amid descending rain and*

> *roaring floods! Trust yourself with Him who will go with you through the dark and surging current of death's stream, who will land you safely on the celestial shore, and who will make you sit with Him in heavenly places forever.*
> —Charles H. Spurgeon, *Morning by Morning*[39]

If we do this, with the help of our great God, then He can use us to do incredibly powerful and miraculous things within the first responder profession. The impact cannot be overstated with a people dedicated to the Lord. We will be different, and that difference will heal and impact our families and communities in godly ways. It won't be easy, but it will be worth it!

Don't forget that,

> *In all these things we are more than conquerors through him who loved us. . . . [and that nothing] in all creation, will be able to separate us from the love of God in Christ Jesus our Lord.*
> —Romans 8:37, 39b

Don't give up.
Pursue Jesus.
No matter what, and come what may.
Following Jesus is the only way to keep the peace within.

> *Jesus spoke to the people once more and said, "I am the light of the world. If you follow me, you won't have to walk in darkness, because you will have the light that leads to life."*
> —John 8:12

39. C. H. Spurgeon, *Morning by Morning* (1865; rev. ed., Abbotsford, WI: Aneko Press, 2020). Used with permission.

PRAYER

Father, I (Clint, the author) am grateful for the person who took the time to read this book. I earnestly pray specifically for the individual reading this prayer. May they decide to follow You above all else! Bring them closer to Your heart and spur them on toward a faithful life of service to You, their family, and the people in their communities. Jesus, I have personally felt and experienced Your kindness, love, and faithfulness. If You pour it out on me, I know You want to do the same for them. Heal them and give them a new life, a new heart, and new desires. Let Your Holy Spirit flow into their life, and light them up for Your glory. Your love for them is so great. Help them feel that love right now in this moment. Thank You, Father, for all You have done, all You are doing, and all You will do. In Jesus's name and by the power of the Holy Spirit, let it be. Amen.

ACKNOWLEDGMENTS

There are so many people who had a hand in bringing this book to life. The amount of help, support, and encouragement from friends and family has been incredible. From the time I made the "random" decision in college to pursue law enforcement as a professional career, to the present day, God has used so many people, situations, and events to shape me into the person I've become. The way God weaves everything into our story for our good and His glory (Romans 8:28) is amazing to me! There's no way I could mention everyone, but I am so thankful to God for those who played any part in assisting me on this journey.

Innovo Publishing has provided their expertise and professionalism in the publishing realm, for which I am very grateful.

Robert Cullom, who has been a great friend and brother in Christ, provided a special recommendation and a very trusted opinion from the first responder community. Jeff Lott, a close brother in Christ who God has used to help me along in my walk with Jesus, has been there to encourage and support me along the way. One of my pastors, who is also a mentor and close friend, Jeff Holland, lent his theological guidance as well as encouragement.

My immediate family has been incredibly supportive, understanding, and encouraging throughout, offering their views from a non-first-responder perspective. My wife's longtime college friend and faithful missionary to Papua New Guinea, Emily Bonner, was the honest and encouraging reviewer I didn't know I needed! I cannot thank her enough for her time and effort in helping me finalize everything. My wife, Amanda, is amazing! The strength she has portrayed for me and many others cannot be overstated. God has blessed me with a godly and loving wife and mother of our children who has been there for me and our family every step of the way. She's been an editor, sounding board, encourager, and constructive critic, and she has graciously let me tell our story. She had my back from the jump and has always been my ride or die partner on this wild journey.

Lastly, but obviously not least in any way, I have to give credit and glory to my Heavenly Father. He has brought me from death to life and continues to change me in so many ways. He deserves all of the glory and honor for the truths you've read in this book. I am simply trying to tell of all He has done in my life so others may see and seek to glorify Him. Thank You, Jesus! I'm so incredibly humbled that You would choose to use me to help others.

www.ingramcontent.com/pod-product-compliance
Lightning Source LLC
LaVergne TN
LVHW090612110826
845146LV00001B/352

* 9 7 9 8 8 8 9 2 8 1 4 5 0 *